Divine Love

Divine Love

The Emblems of Madame Jeanne Guyon and Otto van Veen

VOLUME 1

POETRY BY

Jeanne de la Mothe Guyon

ILLUSTRATIONS BY

Otto van Veen

INTRODUCTION AND TRANSLATION FROM THE ORIGINAL FRENCH BY

Nancy Carol James

FOREWORD BY

William Bradley Roberts

PICKWICK *Publications* • Eugene, Oregon

DIVINE LOVE
The Emblems of Madame Jeanne Guyon and Otto van Veen, Vol. 1

Pickwick Publications
An Imprint of Wipf and Stock Publishers
199 W. 8th Ave., Suite 3
Eugene, OR 97401

www.wipfandstock.com

PAPERBACK ISBN: 978-1-5326-6279-9
HARDCOVER ISBN: 978-1-5326-6280-5
EBOOK ISBN: 978-1-5326-6281-2

Cataloguing-in-Publication data:

Names: Guyon, Jeanne Marie Bouvier de La Motte,—1648–1717, author. | Veen, Otto van, 1556–1629, illustrator. | James, Nancy Carol, translator | Roberts, William Bradley, foreword writer.

Title: Divine love : the emblems of Madame Jeanne Guyon and Otto van Veen, Vol. 1 / Jeanne de la Mothe Guyon ; translated by Nancy Carol James.

Description: Eugene, OR: Pickwick Publications, 2019 | Includes bibliographical references.

Identifiers: ISBN 978-1-5326-6279-9 (paperback) | ISBN 978-1-5326-6280-5 (hardcover) | ISBN 978-1-5326-6281-2 (ebook)

Subjects: LCSH: Guyon, Jeanne Marie Bouvier de La Motte,—1648–1717 | Veen, Otto van, 1556–1629 | Emblems—Early works to 1800 | Love in art | Christian poetry | Religious poetry | Spiritual life—Catholic Church

Classification: N7745.L6 *A25 2019 (print)* | N7745.L6 *(ebook)*

Manufactured in the U.S.A. 03/06/19

Contents

Acknowledgements

MANY PEOPLE HAVE CONTRIBUTED to this volume. I am grateful for the support of Dr. Carlos Eire during my dissertation work on Jeanne Guyon. In particular, I wish to thank G. Richard, Dimler SJ for his excellent scholarship on religious emblems.

I want to thank the parishioners of St. John's, Lafayette Square, Washington, DC for their dialogue about Jeanne Guyon and her rich theology.

Many thanks go to my family, who share my passion for the work of Jeanne Guyon. Roger, Hannah, and Melora have read, explored, and researched Jeanne Guyon along with me. I am grateful that we share this love.

Above all, I think my readers who share a love for Jeanne Guyon and her ideas about interior faith. Guyon's books have been kept alive by those who continue to seek a profound interior life where Jesus Christ lives and moves and has his being. I hope that Guyon's Christian interior faith lives for centuries yet to come.

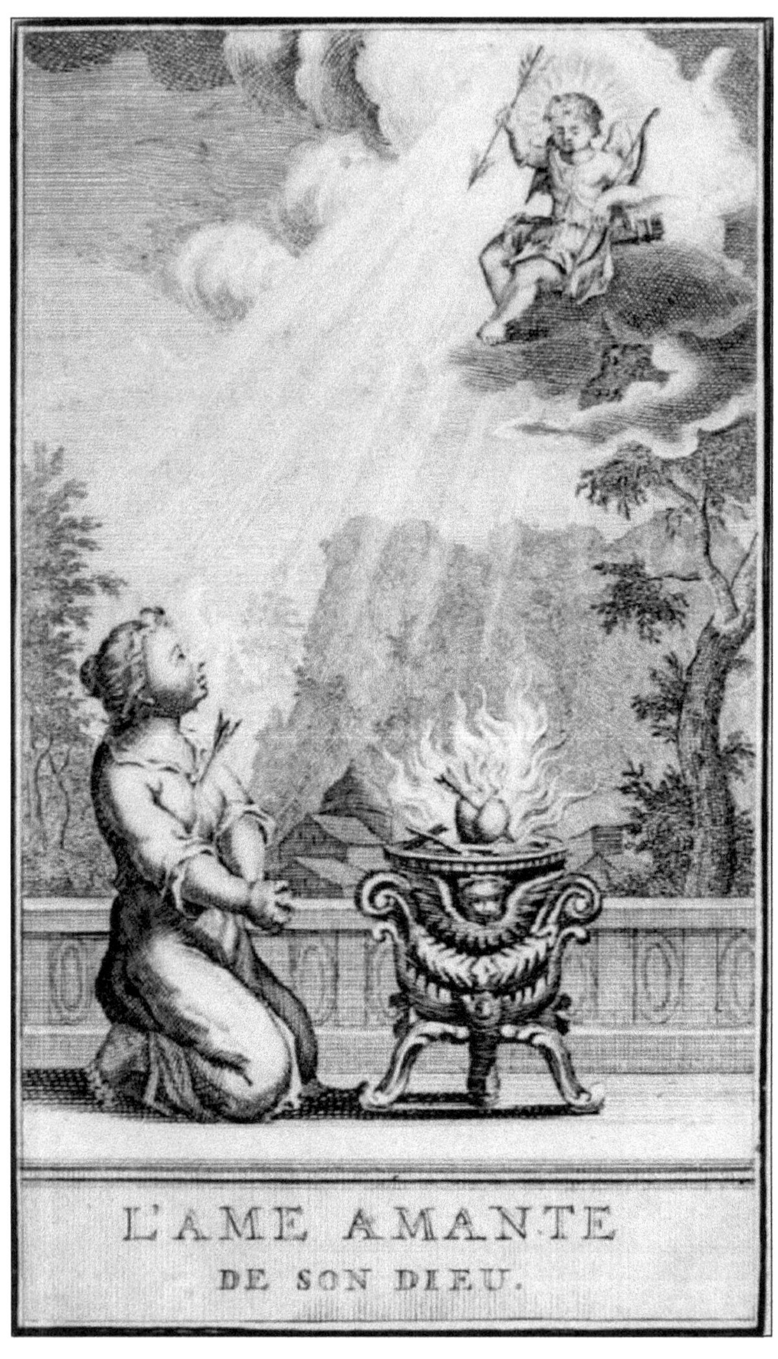

The Soul, Lover of God

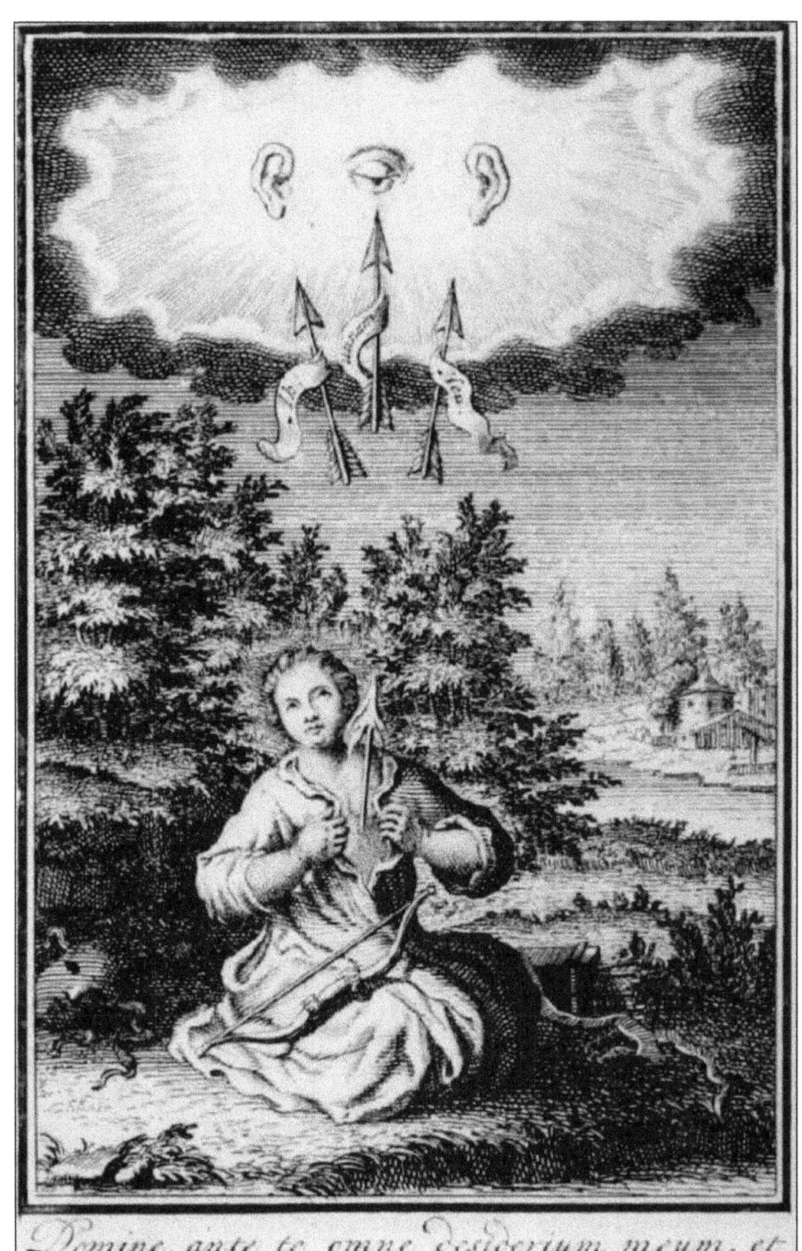

Domine, ante te omne desiderium meum, et gemitus meus à te non est absconditus. Psal. 37.

O Lord, all my longing is before you; my sighing
is not hidden from you. Psalm 38:9

Foreword

EMBLEM BOOKS WERE A literary genre of the Renaissance. This popular form wielded a powerful influence over art, literature, and culture for over two hundred years. The subject matter might be secular or sacred in nature, the latter category often reflecting the concerns of the Catholic Counter-Reformation. Three broad categories of emblem books prevail: material from natural history following the bestiary tradition; episodes from fables, ancient history, or proverbs and other religious subjects; scenes from everyday life. The intent of the books was intellectual delight, or, in the case of Madame Jeanne Guyon, religious devotion.

An individual *emblem* consisted essentially of three parts: *inscriptio* (the motto); *pictura* (the picture); and *subscriptio* (a brief poem).[1] Though examples exist of emblems with up to twelve parts, the three-part emblem came to be the standard form. (An exception, the *naked emblem,* had no pictures.) Typically an Emblem Book contained between ten and one hundred emblems, though examples exist with many more.

Most early books were in Latin, later translated into vernacular languages, chiefly Italian, French, Dutch, German, Spanish, and English. (The present book, then, follows a long tradition of translations.) Symbolism and mystery marked the content of the poetry, though the point was not to present the reader with an inscrutable puzzle so much as to delight with nuance and intellectual challenge.

Living in the waning days of the Renaissance, Madame Jeanne Guyon (1648–1717) was naturally familiar with and attracted to the emblem book genre. Author Nancy James brings to the present book the skill and insight of a seasoned Guyon scholar, having written twelve volumes on the Catholic mystic. Her saturation in the works of Guyon over many years naturally endows James with keen eye and penetrating insight. The reader may expect that she will bring the mystic's poetry to life with accuracy and beauty, and not be disappointed.

1. Much of the historic information comes from Robin Raybould, *The Symbolic Literature of the Renaissance* (Bloomington, IN: Trafford, 2006).

Madame Guyon discovered in Otto van Veen an artist who had visually portrayed the verbal truths that she wished to convey. Van Veen (also called by the Latin forms of his name, Otto Venius or Octavius Vænius) was a Dutch painter and draftsman, active in Brussels and Antwerp in the late sixteenth and early seventeenth centuries. The artist's Belgian years doubtless made him accessible later to Guyon, whose voracious appetite for art and literature would have led her to these engravings. Van Veen himself produced several emblem books, but his place in art history is primarily secured by his having been the teacher of the Flemish master Peter Paul Rubens (1577–1640).

The reader of the present volume is the happy recipient of the abundant riches of the confluence of three inspired artists and intellectuals: Madame Guyon, Monsieur van Veen, and Dr. Nancy James.

William Bradley Roberts, D.M.A.

Virginia Theological Seminary (Episcopal)
Alexandria, VA.
January 19, 2019

Introduction

NANCY CAROL JAMES, PHD

EMBLEMS SEEM LIKE A mystery to our postmodern minds, though twenty-first-century graphic novels resemble emblems with their use of text and images for meaning. Likewise, an emblem combines an image with a text to offer a heightened sense of meaning and purpose. The meanings they create are subtle and profound because of the combination of images and text rather than either of these elements standing alone. In the sixteenth and seventeenth centuries, spiritual emblems were designed as an intervention into human lives. In our natural self, our material eyes are blinded to the spiritual realities surrounding us. When they are opened, we might sense the grandeur of the God and move towards this loving light. Cathedral stained-glass windows exemplify the best examples of religious emblems. The observer through use of imaginative connections understands the ideas of biblical stories and the possibility of spiritual participation in these narratives. Love might flow from the believer's heart to the heart of God. Reciprocated love, Jeanne Guyon calls this, the love that takes the mystery of human life and overwhelms it with happiness of the relating to God. These emblems of *Divine Love* offer this reciprocated love as their meaning. Artist Otto van Veen and author Jeanne Guyon's emblems are distinctive in their revelation of the joyful relationship between Christ and human soul.

This popular seventeenth-century European emblem book, *Divine Love*, offered a fresh and engaging look at the soul's relationship to God, Father, Son, and Holy Spirit. Guyon and van Veen had understood profound truths about Divine Love and offered a way to live the Christian faith in beauty and love. The emblems reveal the Christian life as one of hope and adventure. In these emblems, God stoops to care for people as his children, even when human beings are lost in sin and obstinacy. God gradually transforms the soul into living in joyful and realized holiness. God covenants to be with the soul always. The pictures show a sweet moral environment filled with the grace of the revelation of Jesus Christ. The gentle and humble Christ introduces the soul the glories of spiritual redemption.

The Philosophy of Emblems

Scholarship in recent years has made fascinating discoveries that European emblem books were widely popular in the sixteenth and seventeenth centuries. An emblem book resembles a picture book containing engaging text and helpful images. Guyon and van Veen had an intense desire to communicate meaning, purpose, and truth to readers by using both texts and imagery. The combination of Guyon's text with van Veen's image made a meaning with the purpose of engaging and enlarging the reader's soul. This intensified communicative experience made by the interaction of the poem and image reflects the analogous interaction between Christ and the soul.

The subject of this emblem book describes the human soul as the lover of God seeking union with God. This particular book of emblems was widely popular in the sixteenth and seventeenth centuries and homes from huts to palaces had a copy of it. In a time of rampant illiteracy, if a person wanted to know more about the love of God, they could look at the engravings. If a person could also read, the poems added by Jeanne Guyon added another layer of understanding that could penetrate the person's soul.

How do these emblems work in the engaged reader? In this emblem book, an example is seen in one of the first drawings. In the emblem "Love Penetrates and Sustains" the reader sees an abstract circular object with arrows shooting through this object, penetrating at many angles. The astute reader applies the terms to the image and makes new connections that provoke critical thinking and make new symbols. This particular emblem uses multiple sources to combine and create a new meaning. Some of the ideas and symbols that form the emblem include the following.

- The idea of the mystery of God revealed to the individual soul
- The Roman mythology of Cupid shooting an arrow shot into the heart that creates love
- An analogy between the universe with the human heart and soul
- Essences pour into the opening created by the bow and arrow
- Scripture from 1 Corinthians 2:9 describing the mystery of what God prepares
- God's character might be poured into the openings

Through the work of the imagination, the reader receives a new understanding of spiritual realities. In rational terms, we would say that these emblems on Divine Love invite contemplation, and an increased reception of God in our interior life through imaginative reconstruction of spiritual realities.

Historical Roots of These Emblems

Even a princess can wonder about the experience of Divine Love and one named Princess Isabella Clara Eugenia, the Duchess of Brabant and the Sovereign of the Spanish Netherlands, did just that. She wondered what Divine Love was like: how it looked and felt. She thought about this with such intensity that she wrote a letter to a famous artist in her era, Otto van Veen. The princess asked him to draw pictures about Divine Love. Maybe her question was, how do I spiritually live in the love of God?

The artist Otto van Veen (also known as with his title of honor D'Othon Vaemius 1556–1629) honored her request. As the teacher of Peter Paul Rubens and considered the leading art teacher in Antwerp, he published these in 1615 and they were widely disseminated. Otto van Veen bases his drawings on Scripture and his first illustration begins with a biblical reference reading, "What no eye has seen, nor ear heard, nor the human heart conceived, what God has prepared for those who love him" (1 Corinthians 2:9). He then offered these emblems as examples showing what God might prepare and give to us.

Otto van Veen drew sixty images depicting the soul in many states during a long life's journey. He supplied short phrases of meaning written below each drawing. Otto van Veen shows us God's love in many differing ways. He drew Divine Love as the Child Christ (also called Divine Love), a gentle and humble boy who walks up to the soul, shown as a young girl known as Anima, who lies fallen and hurt in the street. With kindness the Christ greets her and offers her his hand. After she accepts his gracious help, Christ leads the soul through many differing experiences in life. Bonded through this journey, eventually after many shared experiences, the soul and Christ become one, united in love. *Emblems of Divine Love* spread rapidly. This book inspired by the need of a princess and the inspiration of the artist became a popular book throughout Europe.

About seventy years following the publication of van Veen's emblems, another faithful person found his book and added additional text to these images. Madame Jeanne de La Mothe Guyon (1648–1717) added poems about Divine Love to Otto van Veen's sixty drawings. She called the human soul the lover of God. In these poems, Guyon's words soar as she addresses God directly, speaking from her heart to the divine heart.

A popular spiritual author, the French mystic Jeanne Guyon had suffered through many of her own difficulties in life. As a young and wealthy widow, she became embroiled in a church controversy when she refused to give her financial resources to the Roman Catholic Church. After she became a popular author on spiritual topics, Guyon was arrested and suffered through a church inquisition. She endured nearly ten years of incarceration for her beliefs, including five years in the Bastille. In her book *Bastille Witness* she states that on June 4, 1698, when she entered the Bastille, she brought these drawings on Divine Love into the prison. Guyon was eventually cleared of all charges and was released from the Bastille in March 1703. She spent her last years living in a small cottage and welcoming believers from all over the globe who came to talk about the spiritual life. (For more information about Guyon and her theology, see *The Complete Madame Guyon*, Paraclete Press, 2011.)

These emblems are the mature fruit of her years of suffering. In her times of testing, Guyon found Jesus Christ as an infant, yet as the all-powerful God, living with her in the Bastille and bringing contentment to her, despite all the torments and tortures designed to destroy her. In these poems, we see her attitude toward them, for she believed that in her suffering she experienced the truth and power of Jesus Christ.

Christian Narrative in van Veen-Guyon Emblems

The emblems of Otto van Veen and Jeanne Guyon offer a detailed visualization to us of what Divine Love feels and look like. Through their work, we remember Divine Love, a preoccupation of the seventeenth century, that reaches out to remind us—to awaken us to the magnificent reality of love offering a balm to our wounds, courage to meet our challenges, and a fragrance to our relationships.

Guyon meant for these emblems to be enjoyed. She invites the reader to look at the complex and stimulating relationship between the poem and the engraving. The emblems should provide a fresh and comprehensive experience of the Trinity as God lived in interior faith and mystical incarnation.

Guyon's confession of the infant Jesus Christ as the one true and living Lord of heaven and earth might sustain and comfort us, who live over four centuries after her. In her Epilogue, she asks that we not underestimate the power of these emblems and says they bring excellent lessons. She writes that God has revealed to her that these emblems would stir hearts to love him.

> I feel stirring hearts,
> Receiving from the divine character;
> Your pure and naked truth
> Touches us and releases our sighs . . .

Do not believe, faithful people,
That these are only songs:
Under these new figures
Are excellent lessons.

Receive for the Divine Master
From my hand these small presents:
For reward, please let us be,
Simple and little children.

These emblems of *Divine Love* now become available to postmodern readers. These emblems created by Otto van Veen and Guyon symbolically represent spiritual meaning and, as such, offer a gift of revealed strength and purpose to the aware reader. In our age, when love seems almost forgotten, this emblem book uniting Guyon's poetry and Otto van Veen's illustrations give us a long and ravishing look into what might be. What if Divine Love becomes part of the human experience and joins to human souls? Otto van Veen and Jeanne de la Mothe Guyon took this hope into their own souls and reveal to us their vision of the love of God bonding and becoming one with the human soul.

This way of reading and understanding provides a rich and full experience of life. I present this first English translation of these emblems in hopes that they continue to gather our souls together in closer communion with God, as they have done in previous centuries.

The Revd Dr Nancy Carol James

January 9, 2019

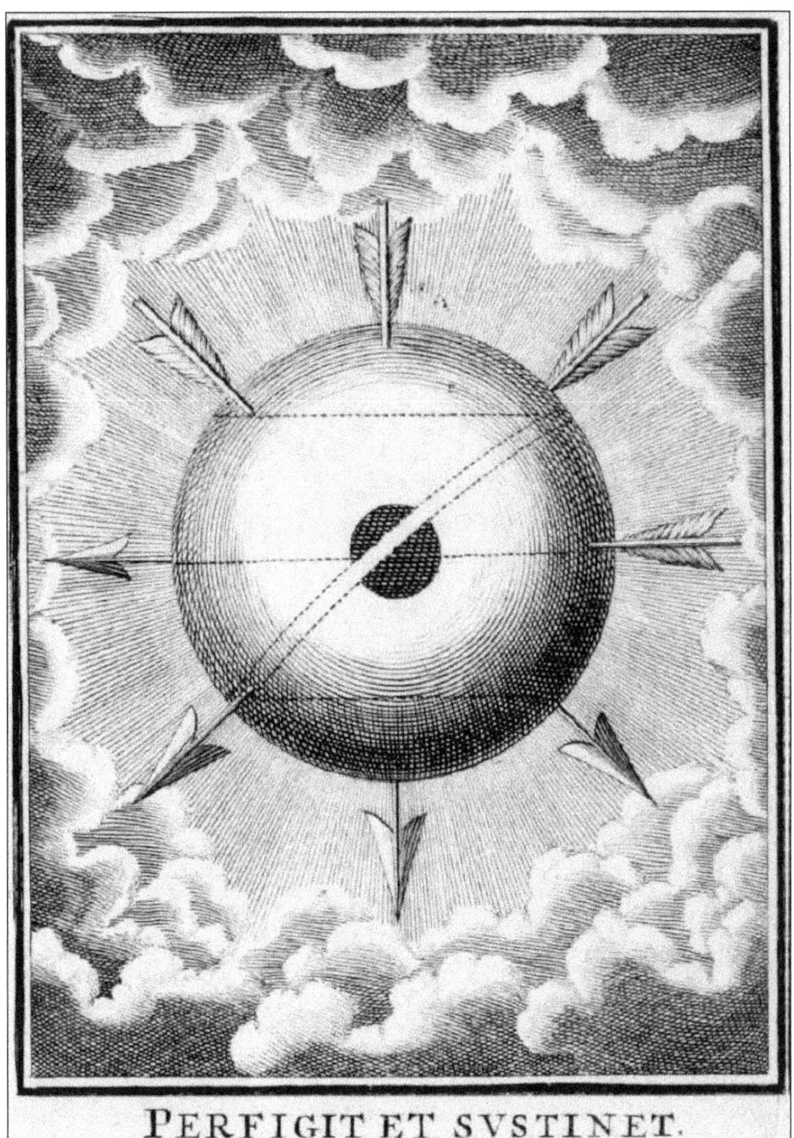

Love penetrates and sustains the universe

A perfectly round circle has been pierced and penetrated by four arrows with the ends of the arrows emerging on the other side. The circle represents the opened divine heart as the essence of the universe.

Love Penetrates and Sustains the Universe

Love, your character penetrates the Universe,
Sustaining your work,
O great God, the universe reveals and testifies to you,
Your creation shows you in many ways.

Certainly, humanity cannot complain
Saying that you hide yourself from our weak eyes.
You know all to whom you have given life.
The eye that desires you sees you everywhere.

The grandeur of your vast beauty,
Ravishing our waiting eyes.
Our faithful heart searches for you,
Finding you in all places.

Poems for the Christ Child

O silent Word made a baby,
O sovereign Lord over the earth and heavens,
Today by grace reveal to us
Your spiritual immensity hidden from our eyes.

I see an infant who is the supreme God;
A revelation beyond our reason:
In his infancy, we see
The King of Zion.

Hiding your brilliance and covering your grandeur
Under the weakest appearance
You win our hearts:
And overcome our resistance.

Second Poem for the Christ Child

Divine infant, who merits
The adoration of the world,
After all your kindnesses
Still no one here seeks you?

We live in eternal forgetfulness
Of your favors and of you:
I suffer to see that today
Almost no one loves you.

We pass by your generosity
In the darkest ingratitude:
Christ Child, the delicacy of heaven,
It distresses me that
I am unable to find a heart
Engulfed by your flames,
Possessed by you,
Loving to the depths of the soul.

Infant so charming and so sweet,
Ah, put everything into your kingdom!
My heart is all yours.
I respond to what you desire.

The water of Shiloh, so calm and tranquil,
By a frightful misfortune
Was frozen one day, and its helpful liquid became
Transparent rocks without grace.
The absence of the Sun turned the spring into solid ice:
Horror filled this former abode.
But the divine Sun by its kind return,
Melted the hardness:
Making in my spirit a delectable calm
And I find peace in my heart.

Prologue

We represent here the charming relationship
Of Love and her Lover;
Their mutual caresses
As sweet as tenderness!

I see on one side of life pains, sorrows,
The liberating dangers, sadness, and tears;
I also see combats, the abyss, shipwrecks,
Winds, tempests, and storms.

But what reduces all these many torments?
In a contentment that surpasses my verses,
The Bridegroom seems jealous of his very chaste
Spouse;
She is also jealous for her Bridegroom;
She wears his yoke which is sweet
From the hand of the Bridegroom
And fatal anxiety
Does not disturb her solitude:
One-on-one with God, as an innocent pleasure!
The loveliness, the sighs!
Everything finally ends in perfect union,
That comes from complete defeat of the
Senses, reason, and will;
All is reduced to unity.

Divine Love, you make this grand work;
It is you, it is you, giving the soul the advantage
To please her celestial Bridegroom,
And to taste the sweet goodness.

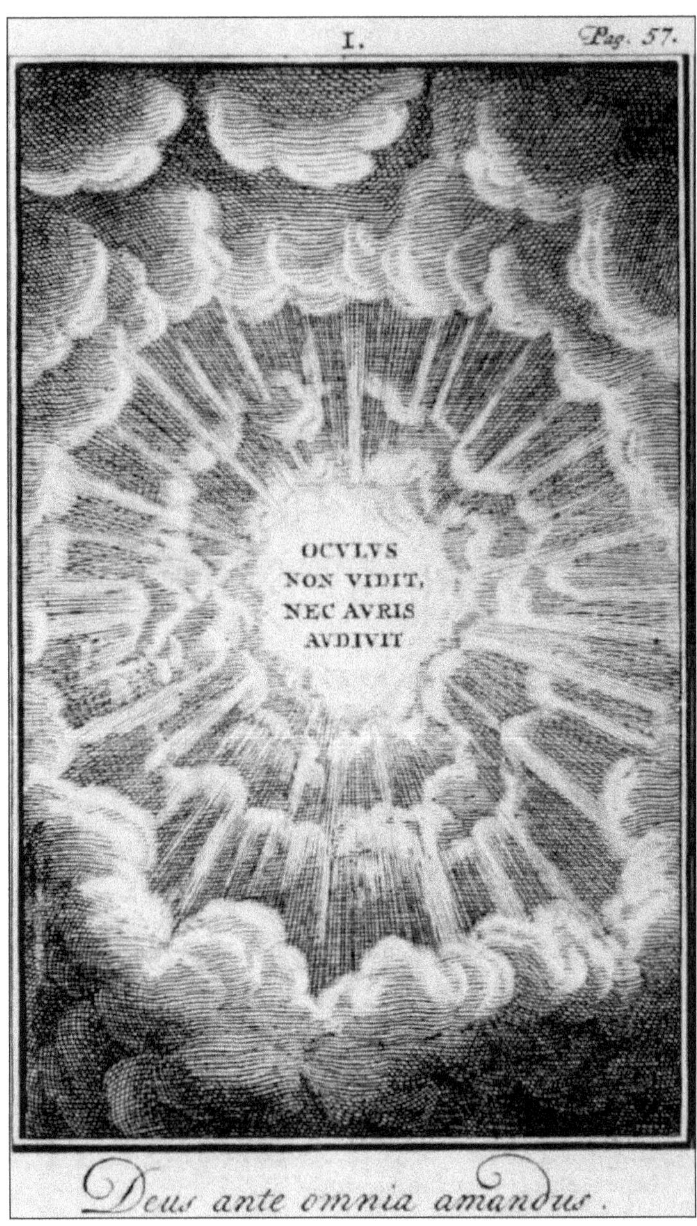

We must love God above all

Clouds surround the empty interior circle where is written, "What eye has not seen, and ear has not heard" 1 Corinthians 2:9. The clouds symbolize a heavenly host serving the divine.

Emblem 1

We must love God above all

The heart of God opens.
The soul lover strengthened,
Captivated by your beauty,
Finds your glorious love
And generous goodness that
Amazes the eye and ear
Of the understanding heart.

My good above all,
My heart asks only for you,
When you love
Nothing else claims me.

My trembling heart,
Enlightened by faith,
In luminous poverty
Abandoning itself
Adores this Good,
Contented in well-being.
I am happy in You
Speaking in quiet.

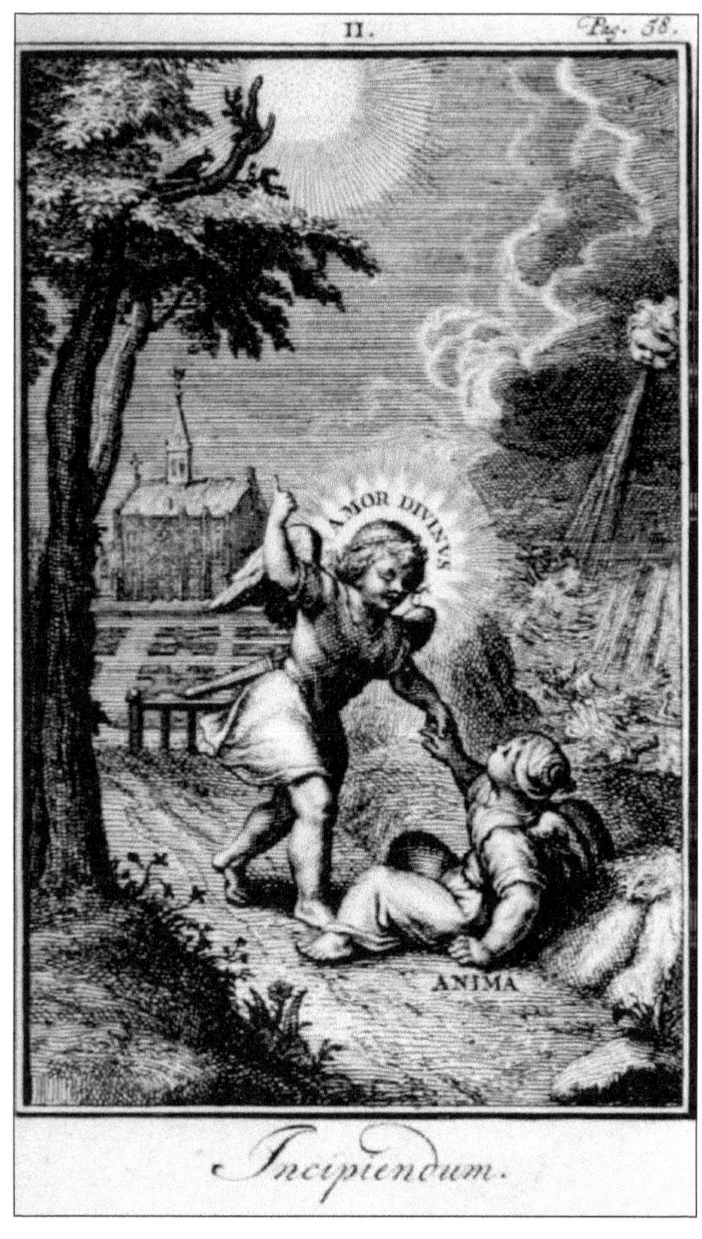

We need to begin

A young boy known as Divine Love or Christus (the Latin form of the name Christ) reaches out to the soul called Anima, a young girl, who has fallen in the road. Behind her a face blows a tempest of wild winds that cause shipwrecks on an ocean.

Emblem 2

We need to begin

I hurt,
I die,
Buried in misery,
Overwhelmed by my sins.
My loving Father,
Touch my evils,
With your healing hand!
Open my eyes, destroy my chains.
End my misery and make me happy.
You ask only my consent.
Yes, I ask this,
Your kindness, so tender and touching,
Ends my torment,
My pride harms me,
For I see my ingratitude.
Lord, show your power.
Tear me open!
I am yours.

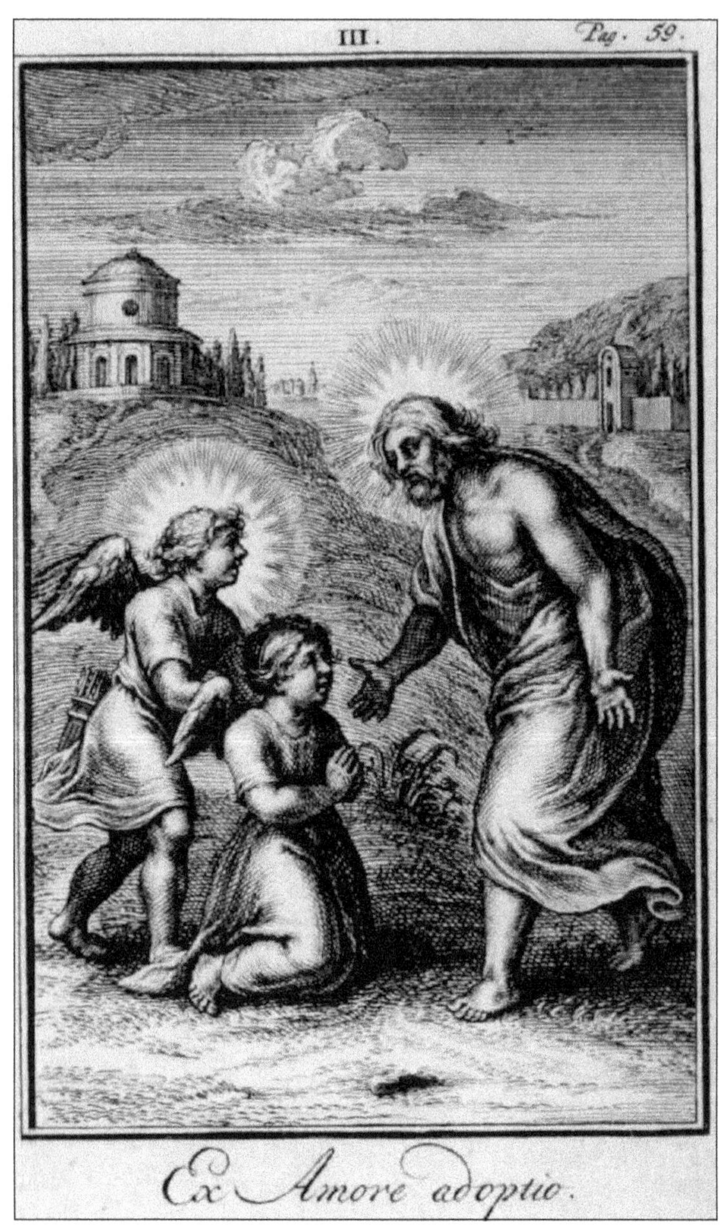

Adoption comes from love

Divine Love introduces the kneeling Anima to God the Father who graciously leans over and reaches out his right hand to her. Both Divine Love and the Father are surrounded by sun-like halos.

Emblem 3

Adoption comes from love

Christ presents me to his Father.
The Father receives me because of his Son's favor;
The Son treats me as his brother,
And shares with me his victory.

Happy adoption, I share Christ's inheritance
Who ends the vile slavery of the devil.
Christ gives me the right to share with
The only heir of the holy Zion!

The Father gives the Son to save me, a slave,
The Son gives himself and makes me redeemed,
The Holy Spirit unites the divine gathering.
I am the newly adopted child of the Father!

Oh, Mystery of Love, showing us,
That the divine All descends on earth for the nothing
Of humans for he is God!
  Be quiet, my Reason, remain in silence,
In this time and place,
Let us speak only in gratitude.

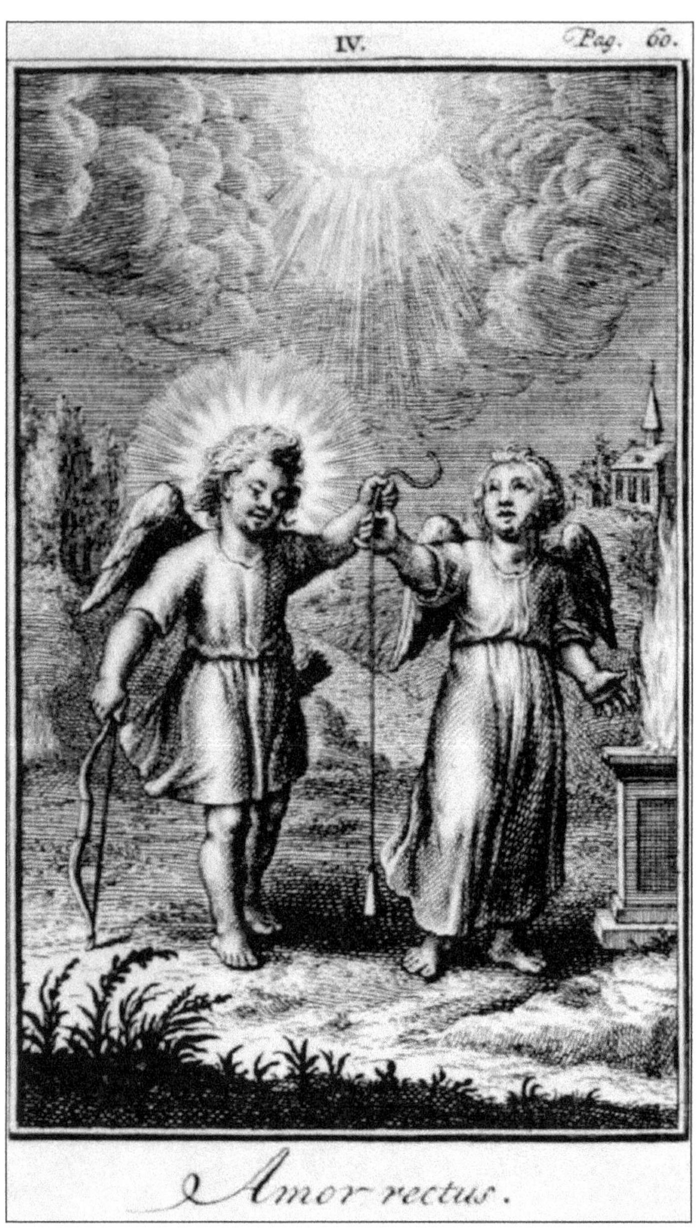

Love is right

Divine Love and Anima share the same shepherd's crook, while to the right a large flame of fire shoots straight up. Anima raises her eyes to heaven, where clouds surround the sun.

Emblem 4

Love is right

Christ opens my human heart
To share with me
His pure will and righteousness.
Simple love opens the door to sovereign Love.

Some desire Love on the earth,
While some fall away from it.
Some look to faith only for support,
Without becoming a sincere lover.
When my heart loves purely,
I move constantly toward God:
All the rest disappoints,
  Light as broken glass.

Love alone balances our hearts,
And helps us choose.
Give my heart, great God, righteousness;
Then with no preference or anxiety,
I remember your goodness makes
Truth my unique companion.

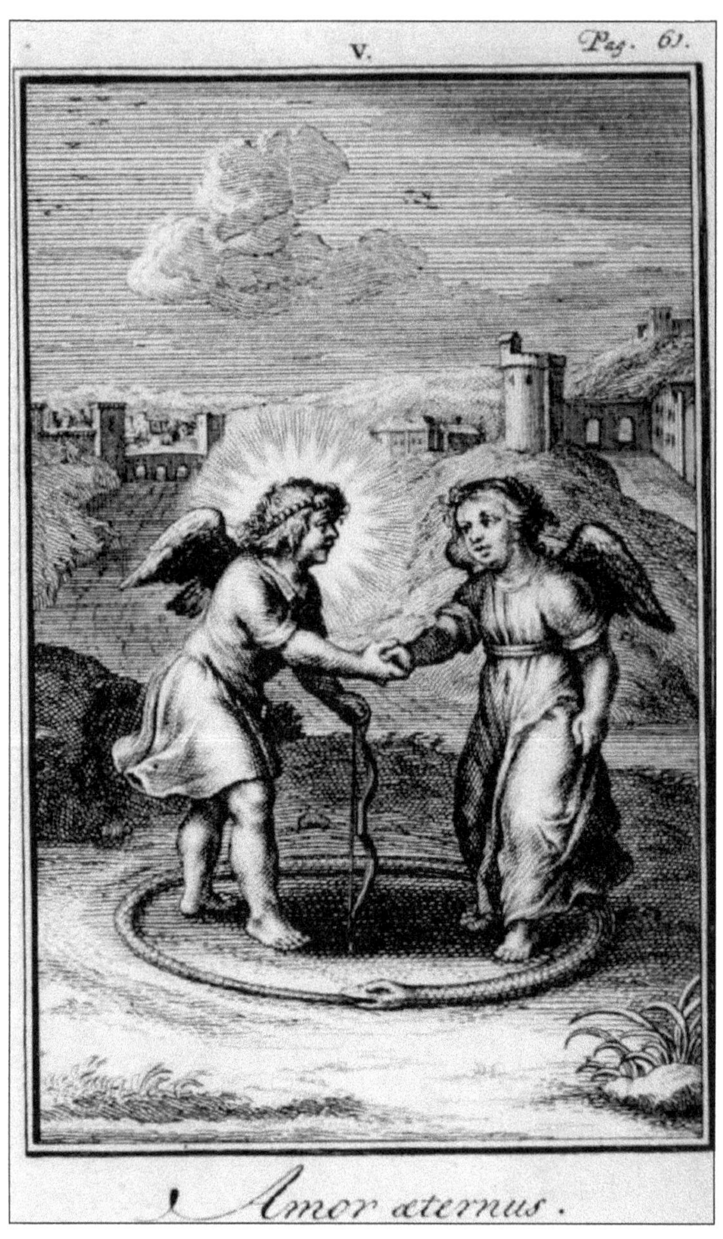

Love is eternal

Facing each other, Divine Love and Anima stand within a circle made by a snake's head eating its tail, a symbol of eternity. Leaning on his bow, Divine Love reaches out to Anima and their right hands join.

Emblem 5

Love is eternal

We happily love you,
Your Love is eternal.
Everything not you in the world,
Is as inconstant as the wave.

The pleasures of this world disappoint like a shadow,
The honors and the goods fly away like the wind:
You remain eternal and unchanging,
Whatever you give lasts:
And when a young heart loves you
You reward her sighs by happy returns.

Your Love has no weakness and fear,
Full of sincerity and not feigned:
When you enflame, I feel the fire;
Filling the center of my heart.

This reciprocated Love continually touches,
Constantly and eternally circling,
Grand, holy, and victorious,
I am eternally, blessedly happy.

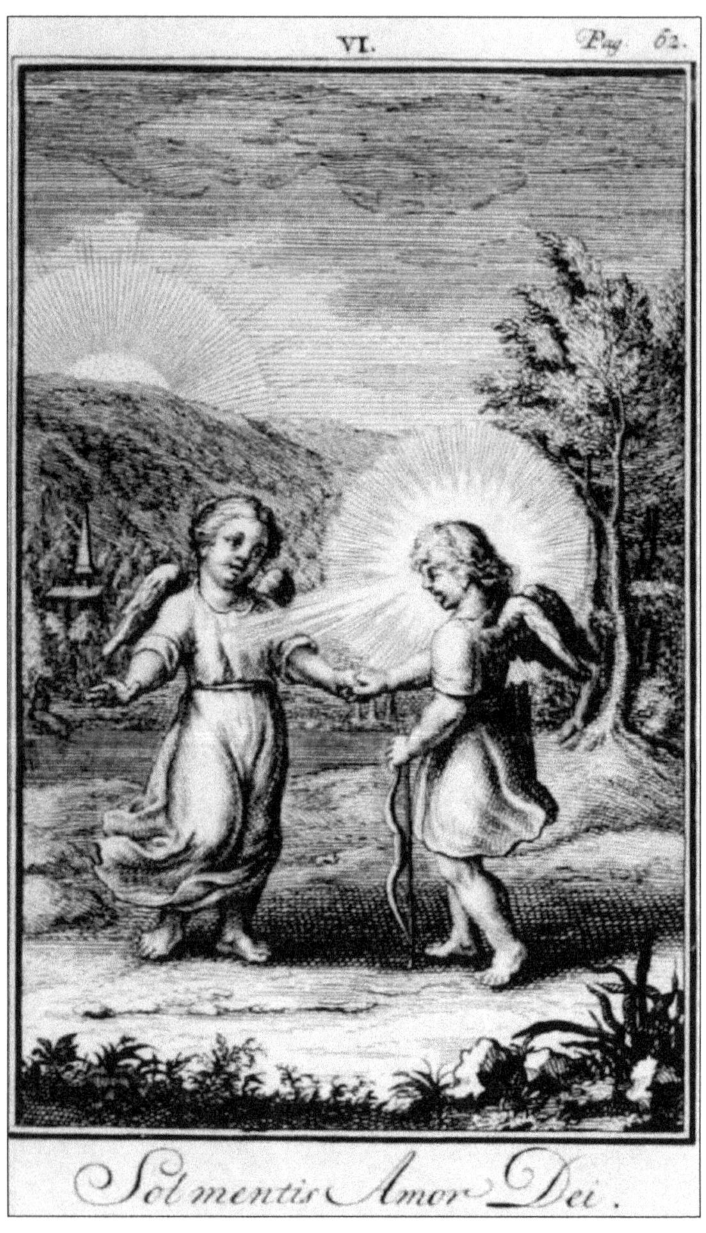

The Love of God is the sun of the soul

Surrounded by a brilliant halo, Divine Love shoots light from his eyes to Anima's heart. She receives this with joy and wonder. Seen over a mountain-top behind, the sun rises with the same shape as the halo.

Emblem 6

The Love of God is the sun of the soul

Dear bridegroom of my heart, your thoughts
Shine on me, filling my soul:
Be my only savior,
I burn forever in your sweet flame!

You charm my heart with inspiration.
I find happiness in your whole kingdom!
I adore your rigor with me
That makes me deny myself.

I want more! Nothing but you! Erase all selfishness!
I feel elevated by a noble boldness:
Remove anything not of you!
In you only I find hope,
Content to have you as king,
I view with scorn all the world.

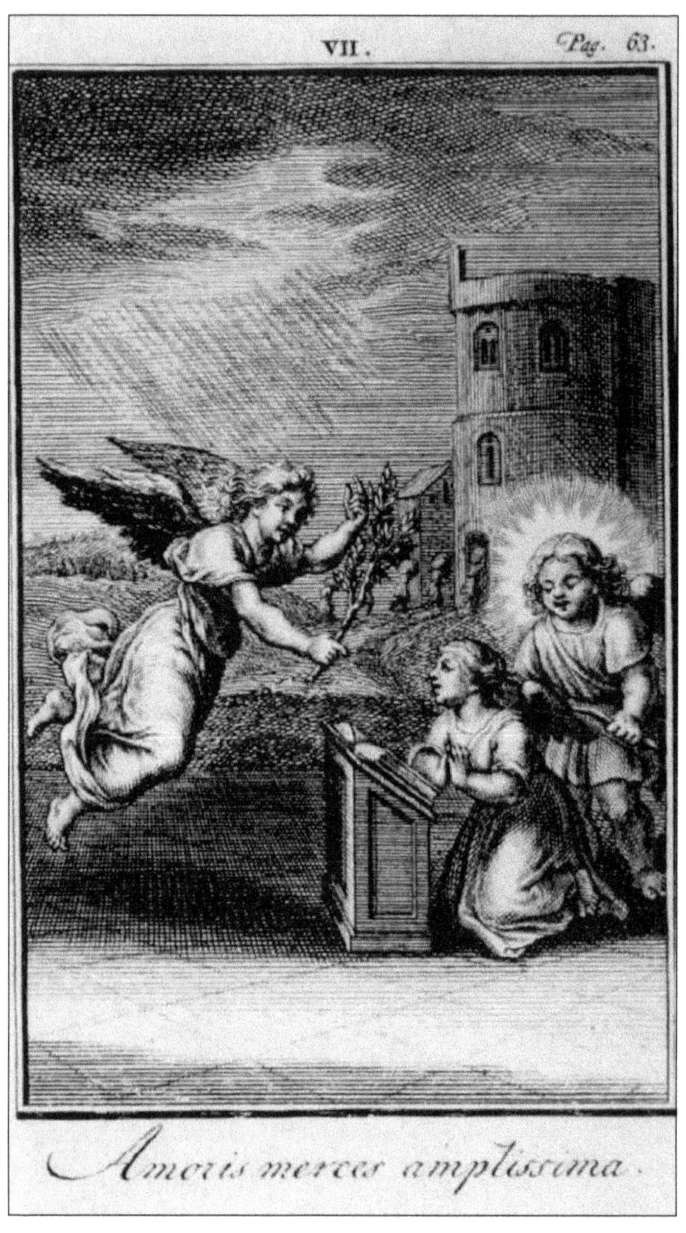

Loves fills with a great reward

An angel comes, offering an olive branch to the praying Anima. Divine Love stands behind her holding his bow with two hands. Diffused light streams through the clouds near a castle tower in the background.

Emblem 7

Love fills with a great reward

The angel speaks, "I tell you, fortunate Lover,
What will one day be your happiness!
What an admirable destiny
God gives those who give him their heart:
You give him yours, he gives himself;
He is your Creator, and his great Love
Makes you his debtor."

Oh, the wonderful reward!
A day of God's presence,
An eternal joy.
Connecting with the Divine
Whom the Angels revere,
God grounds our happiness,
Pouring on us hope and contentment.

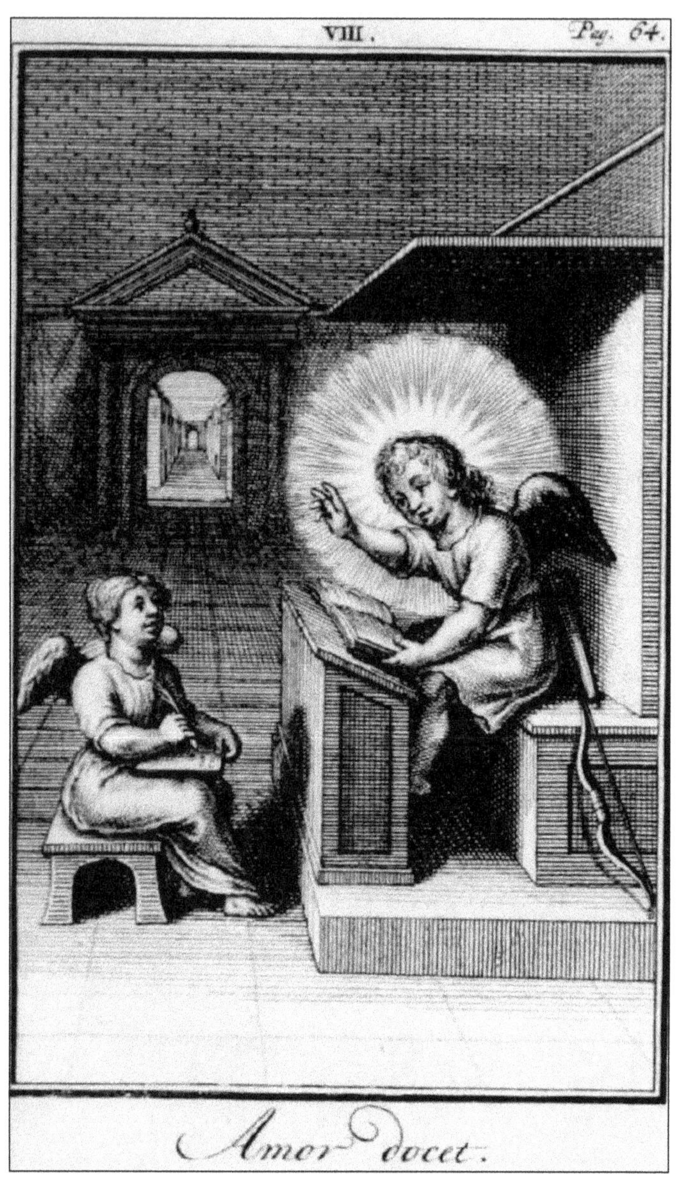

Love instructs

Listening raptly to the instructions of Divine Love, Anima sits on a short bench taking notes. Divine Love instructs from a lectern holding an open book with his bow now resting behind him. He holds his right hand high in a joint sign of instructing and blessing.

Emblem 8

Love instructs

Teach me, my divine Master,
To accomplish your will:
Eternally I will be yours
Docile to the laws prescribed by your kindness.

This incomparable doctrine
Contains all that is sacred and divine;
My heart becomes a tablet
Engraved on by your divine hand!

This law teaches us to leave all things,
To follow the Lawgiver,
These sacred teachings that Love offers us
Are strong, sweet, and real.

Who follows these laws has life
That overcomes death:
Love tests our strength
And we become worthy of envy;
My divine Master
Gives us endless happiness.

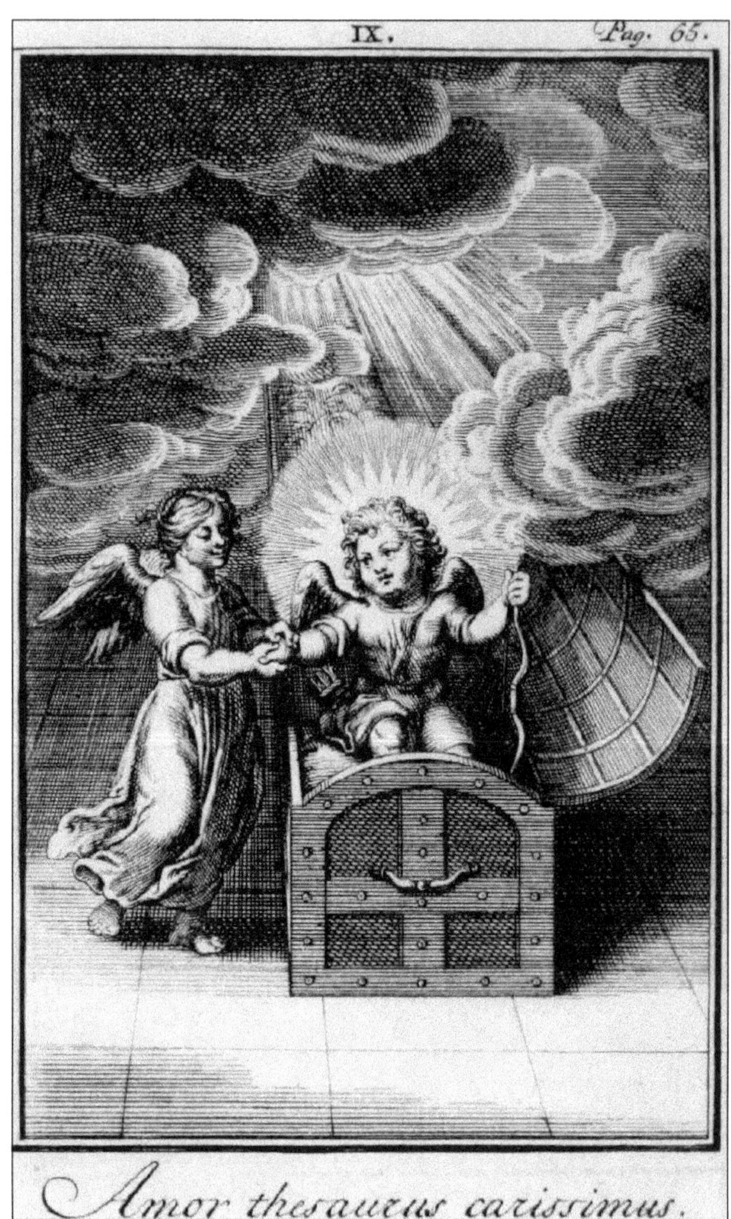

Love is a very dear and precious treasure

Surrounded by a glorious halo, Divine Love sits in a treasure chest, holding his bow in his left hand. Happily, Anima greets and holds him by his right hand. In the background, powerful clouds swirl, but the light rays continue to shine.

Emblem 9

Love is a very dear and precious treasure

Where our treasure is, there will our heart be also:
If our treasure is God, God alone is our richness.
In God we taste special happiness,
Possessed by true wisdom.

The world deceives us with charms,
That tickle the spirit, leaving us empty.
Divine Love gives favors,
With charming and strong sweetness.

The world promises everything yet gives us nothing:
Jesus gives us all things;
We find in him the true good.
The world has more thorns than roses.
You are, O my God, my precious treasure.
To any other, I close my eyes.

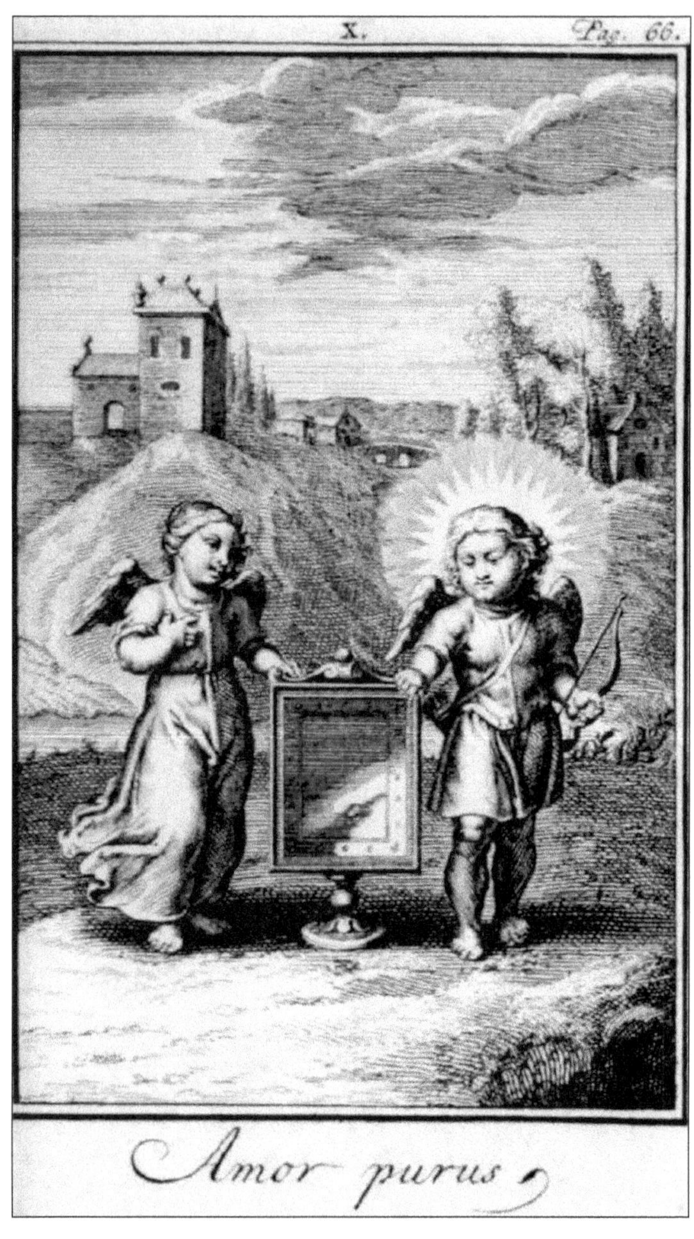

Love is pure

Anima and Divine Love stand on either side of a mirror in an elaborate frame reflecting the surrounding hills and pastoral countryside. In wonder Anima rests her right hand on her heart.

Emblem 10

Love is pure

Seek only the truth.
In divine love we know purity,
Look in the mirror of pure charity,
This is the faithful portrait:
When we make a holy use of pure Love,
We see all things as they surely are.

Everything not of God is false.
Avoid sin and all defilement,
The least stain spoils the beauty.
A breath prevents the image
And mars our perfection:

In love we have God himself.
We participate in pure Love and
Everything unites. There is only God,
God for us, all God, in all places.

Seeing with eyes of faith,
Love all pure, strong hope,
With active charity, we enter
The soul of the King.

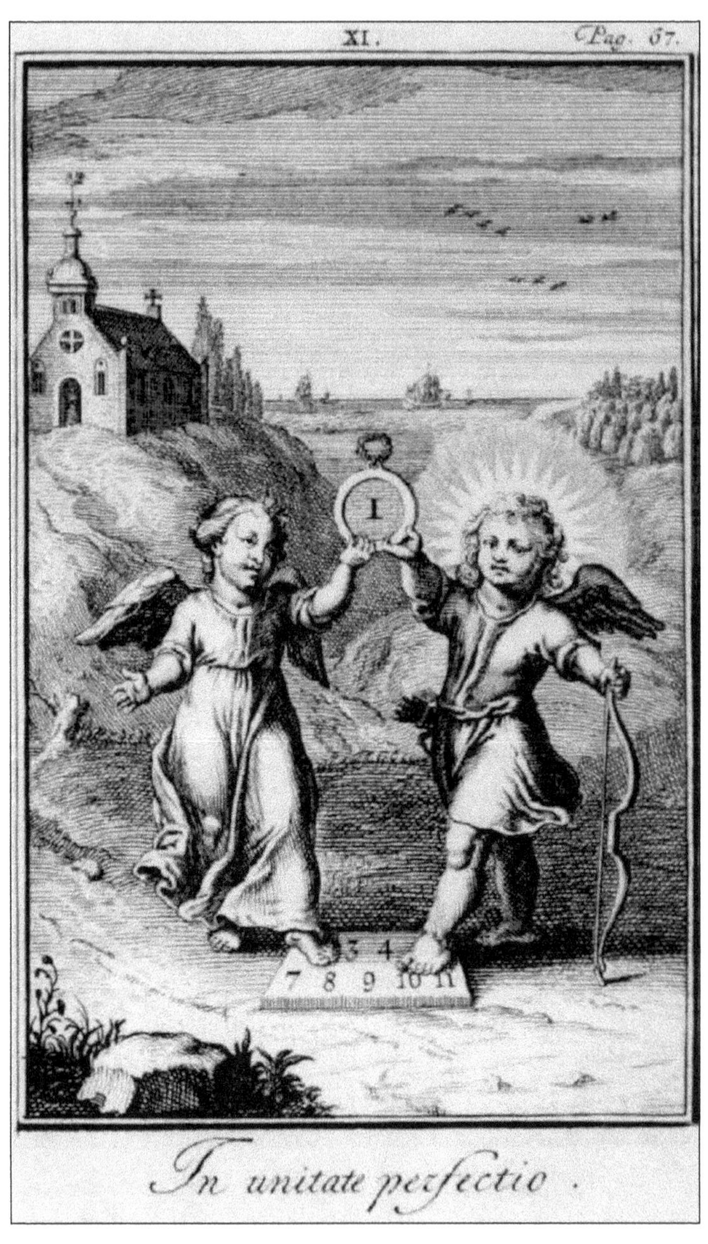

In unity is perfection

Together Divine Love and Anima hold a ring with a heart on the top with the Roman numeral I in the middle. Anima's and Divine Love's left feet rest on a plaque with numbers 1–11 on it.

Emblem 11

In unity is perfection

Holy Love unites,
Simple and true;
Without division
Reducing all to unity.

In God all things are one,
Outside of God we suffer,
Division, troubles, and misfortunes!
Calm and happiness are only in the union.

Jesus asks his Father to help his own family;
He gives divine calm to his friends.
Wonderful Unity, the One Essential!
Jesus, you establish our hearts in God:
You return sweetness for our pains,
Lighten our most difficult work:
You break the chains of the captives,
You give us pleasure in our evils.

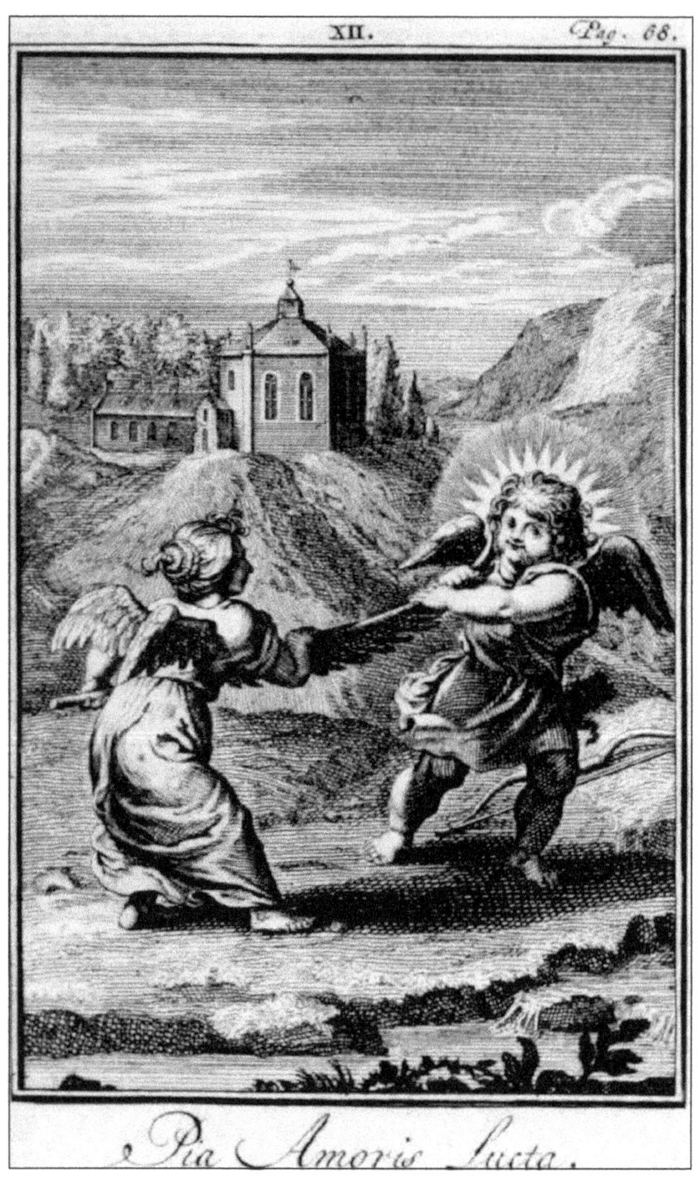

Love has its divine combat

Divine Love and Anima pull against each other as they hold opposing ends of a giant feather or quill. Surrounding their combat are cracks and crevasses in the ground signifying an earthquake. Hills, mountains, and a building with a waving flag are seen behind their struggle.

Emblem 12

Love has its divine combat

What appears to my eyes?
Is this action on earth, or is it from heaven?
Who will win?
Will the conqueror have all the glory?
I know not what to think of this new battle,
Who is the Captain, and who is the soldier?

If I could enter this celebrated duel,
I find my happiness in my captivity.
This divine Conqueror deserves
Our celebration of his glory.
But if I remain victorious,
He becomes my captive and I win his heart;
Losing against him, I gain my victory:
Victor or vanquished, he has all the glory.

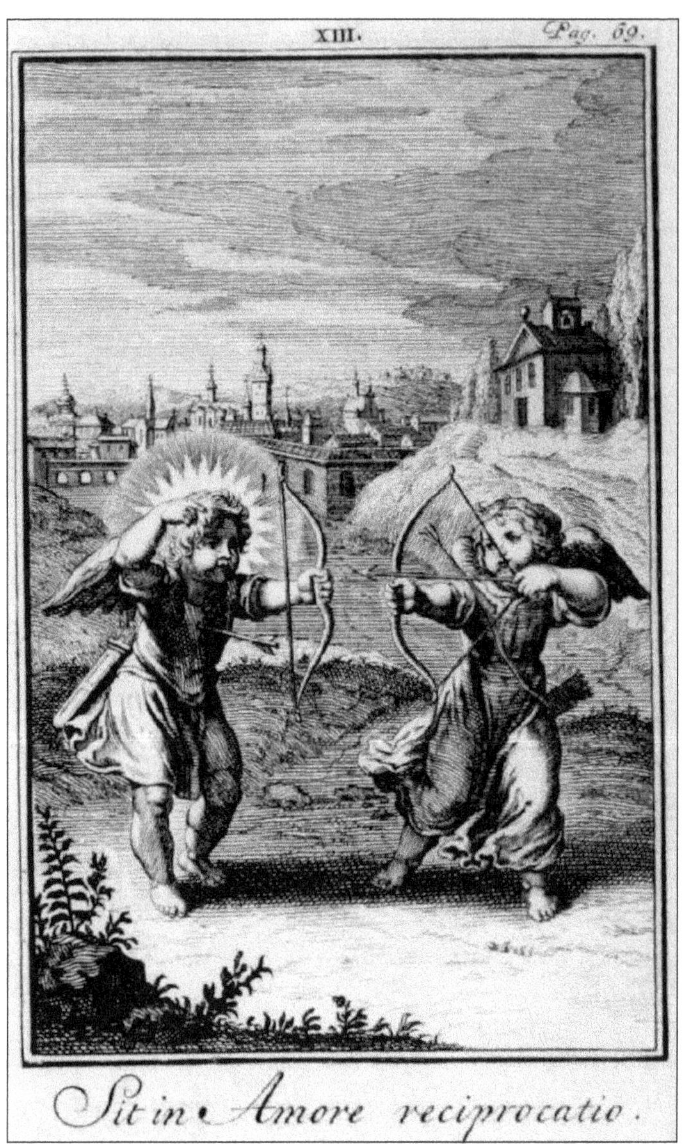

Mutual love

The combat continues with Anima shooting arrows at Divine Love. Divine Love has suffered a direct, penetrating arrow that sticks painfully out of his chest. Anima has another arrow ready to shoot, yet Divine Love does not. Standing with taut muscles in his legs, Divine Love points his right index finger directly at her, instead of a ready arrow.

Emblem 13

Mutual love

What do I see? Love wounds his lover,
And is wounded in return.
The heart pierced by Love's character and smiling face,
Seems content,
And receives new character poured into her by Love.

If these blows are deadly
That death is kind!
And if not deadly,
It would be desirable
To receive these blows
So charming and so sweet!

Love, may I have your same wounds?
The blows that come from your hands,
In spite of my harsh pain,
Are for my heart a sovereign balm.

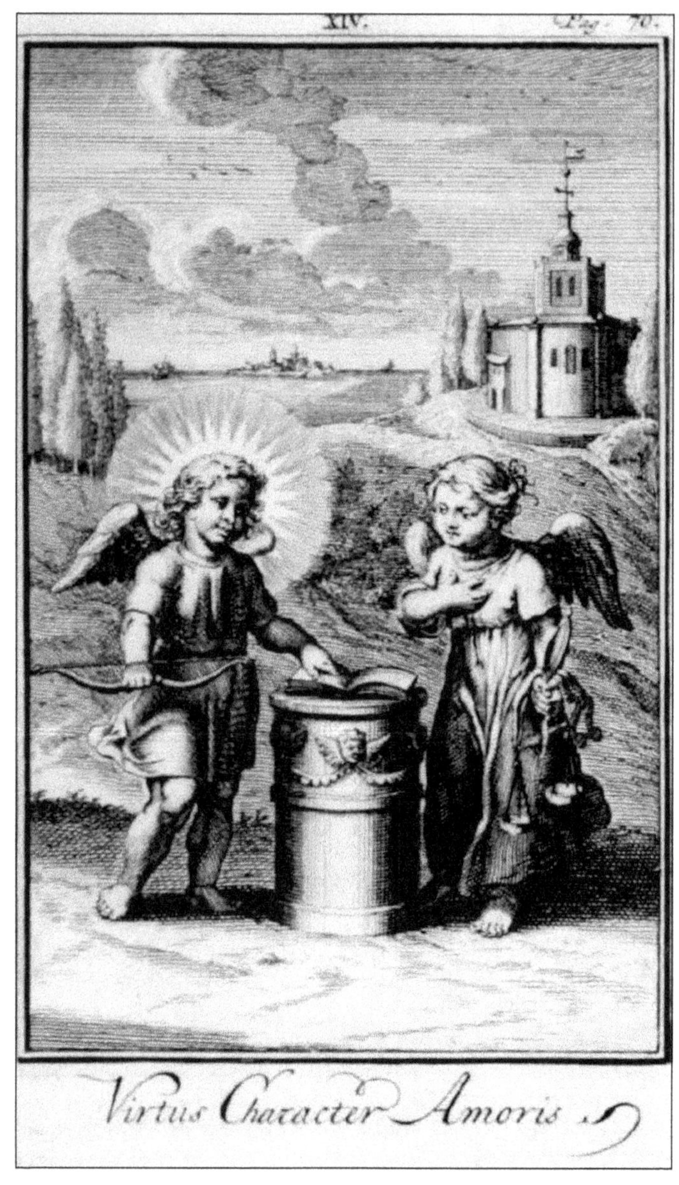

Virtue is the character of Love

Peace reigns between them as Divine Love points to an open book on the top of a short round lectern and Anima places her right hand over her heart. With a sculptured image of Divine Love decorating the front of the lectern, his bow is now in rest position facing downward.

Emblem 14

Virtue is the character of Love

Love is the source of all virtues.
Giving birth to them in our hearts
Just as the sun gives birth to a thousand flowers
In its brilliant race.

The fire of holy Love by its warmth
Produces in us strength and prudence,
Justice and temperance,
Chastity and humble sweetness.

Love crowns the virtues,
And grounds them:
If we want virtue, love sincerely,
Since love gives virtues.

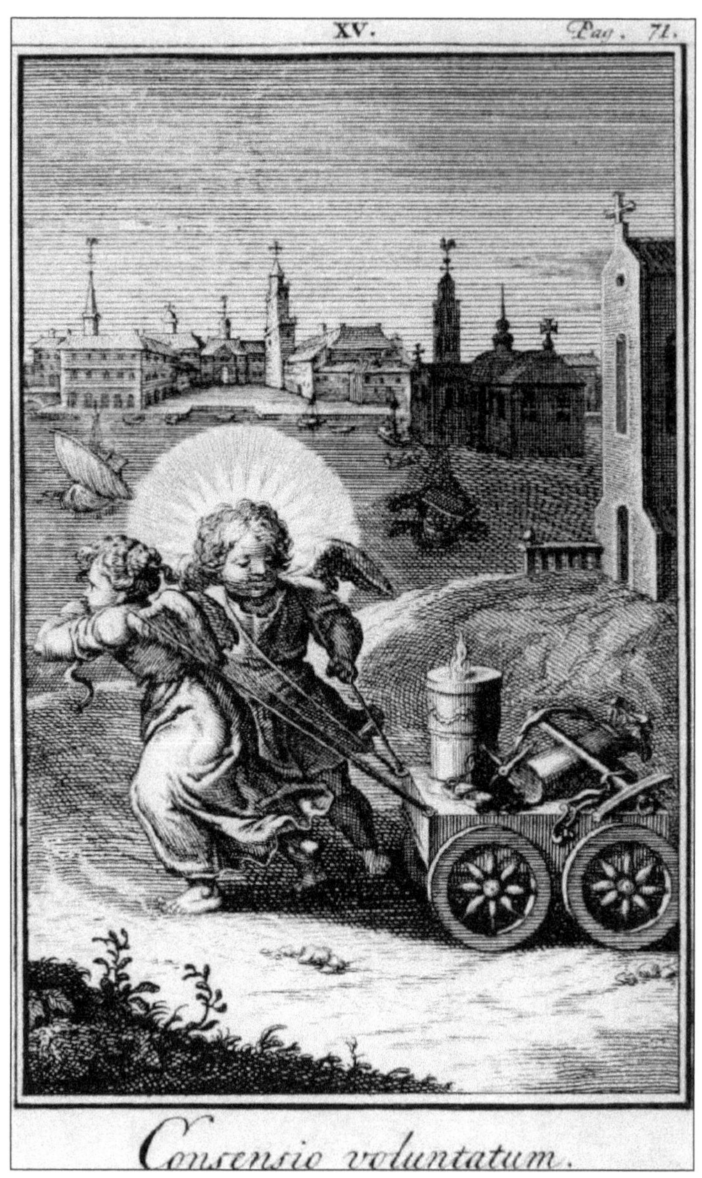

The support of two united wills

Anima struggles to pull a heavy cart holding a round altar with a lighted flame, an anchor, judgment scales, and a full quiver of arrows. Divine Love coaches her and assists her with her load. Leaning fully into her harness, Anima's face now shows serious determination and strenuous effort.

Emblem 15

The support of two united wills

Our wills join
And our desire unite.
A sincere obedience
Is our innocent pleasure!

When we live in dependence
On the supreme Will,
We find his prompt help
In the care given by his kindness.

The heaviest burden becomes a light load
When assured of such assistance.
Far from dragging away our days
In sad misery,
We find even in the midst of torments
Sweet contentment.

Perfect love does not count pain.
What we do for our King;
And his divine Will
Is always our law:
With no fatigue or discomfort,
Everything yields to love and faith.

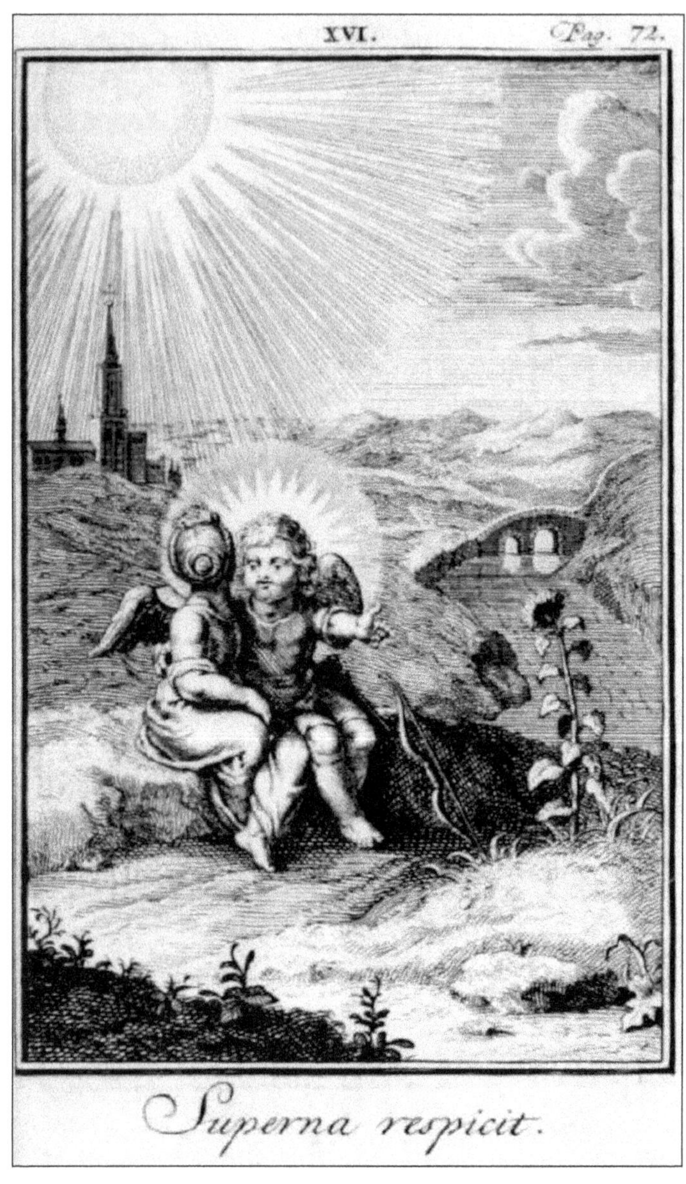

Looking on high

In a scene of happy intimacy, Anima and Divine Love sit on the ridge of a hill talking. Divine Love gesticulates while Anima looks toward the bright sun with long rays beaming directly on a church and the entire scene. In the foreground a sunflower faces the sun with the same angle as Anima's turned head.

Emblem 16

Looking on high

Perfect love like the flower
Turns constantly to the Supreme Beauty:
Without turning to see myself,
I see only God who has my heart.

This sunflower constantly follows the sun's course,
Like this docile soul who
Always follows the divine Will
As its strength and refuge:

Never does the sunflower turn away
To stop the view:
This soul stretches through all her days
Soaring to heavenly truth.

God alone is pleasure and richness,
God touches me:
I see easily and
I find solid wisdom.

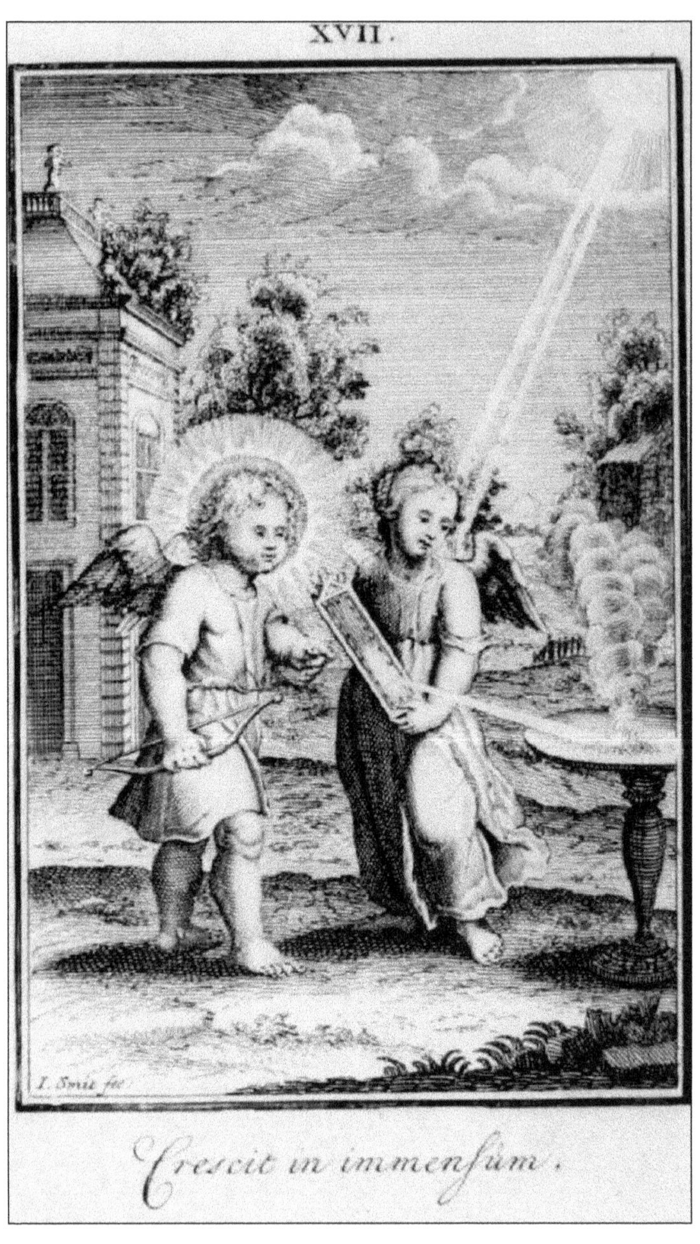

Increases without limit

Reflecting light shines from the sun to a mirror that Anima holds onto a round pedestal which sparks fire. Still carrying his bow, Divine Love points to the fire, which billows up into symmetrical and full flames.

Emblem 17

Increases without limit

When the heart as a pure ice,
Receives the impression of the divine Sun,
Fire grows without measure;
And this unparalleled fire
Full of charming sweetness,
Burns peacefully without pain:
The soul is happy and content
In the midst of the greatest ardor.

Divine Love, O your sweet flame,
Consumes my soul!
Not sparing my heart
You reduce it to a cinder,
Is there anything more tender
Than your holy rigor?

You cleanse me of all that is contrary,
You embellish and fill me with peace,
You take me out of a state of deformity,
Perfectly you please:
O infinite happiness of the sovereign Love!
So in my heart your fire grows eternally.

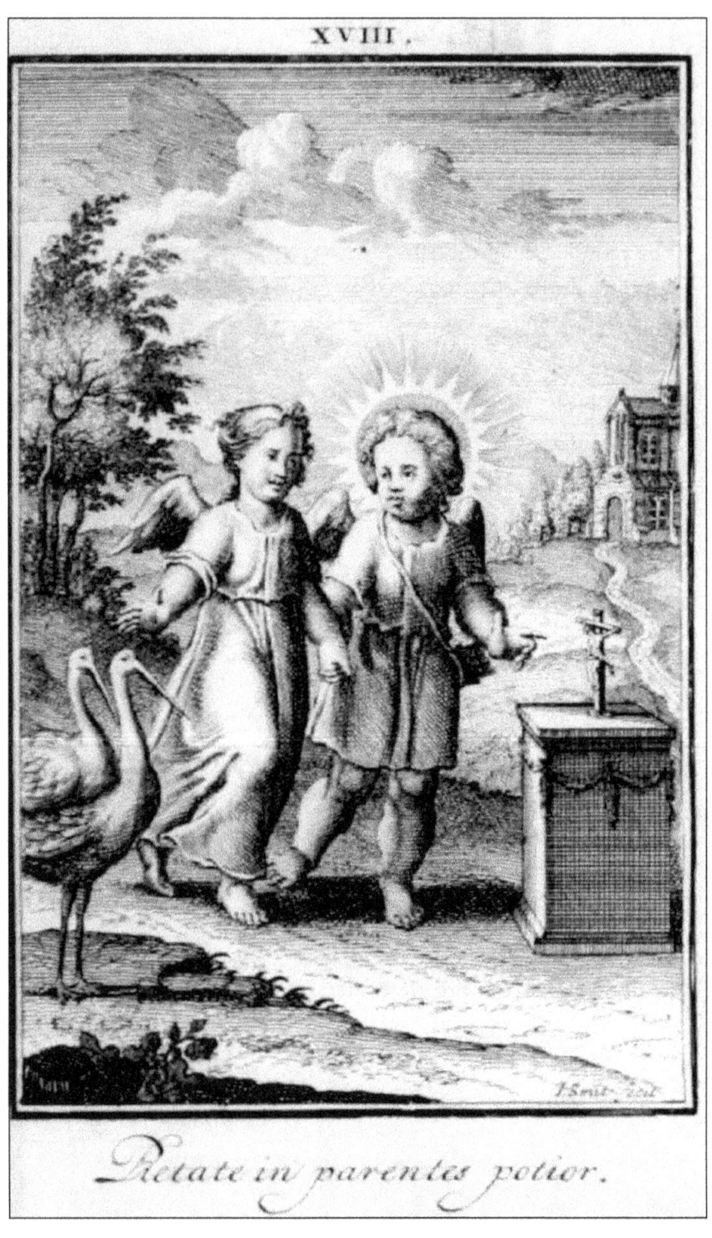

Love better than that of father and mother

Anima's right hand makes a motion pushing aside two storks, who symbolize distracting people. Divine Love holds her left hand and points to a small square altar on which rests a crucifix of Jesus.

Emblem 18

Love better than that of father and mother

Divine Love speaks:

It is not for you
To idolize even father and mother,
Those who do never can please me
Or give me evidence of faith.
But whoever for my Love
Abandons everything,
Deserves the crown and
The eternal home.

The Soul speaks:

If I still want to gain,
Friends, property, and parents, alas, this triple knot
Overwhelms me with misery,
And makes me unworthy of God.
But if I leave everything
To follow my Jesus dying on the cross
Then he is my way and end.
This right choice
Crowns me with his gifts, and crowning I gain
Perfect and unlimited happiness.

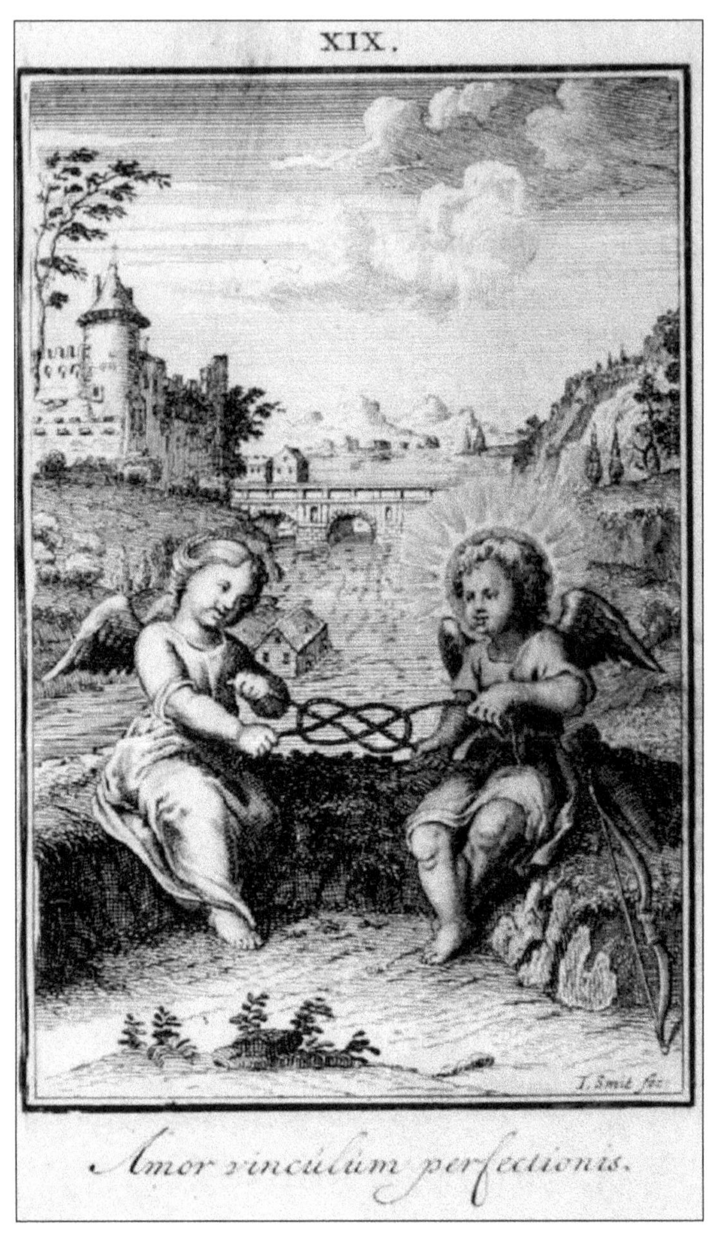

Love is the perfect connection

Anima and Divine Love braid knots together with each holding one end. Their nodes appear perfectly balanced by the cooperative relationship between them.

Emblem 19

Love is the perfect connection

These charming and precious knots
Unite the soul
With the sovereign Lord of earth and heaven
Making us blessed.

This sacred knot unites Love with the lover,
With an overflowing charity!
The lover participates in happiness
Both in time and eternity.

This chain is beautiful
Since it is eternal!
Let us therefore bind these charming links,
These unchanging and divine braids.

We desire these sacred and sweet knots
That bond us with
Our divine Spouse,
Oh, that they are preferred
To all the world of goods and charms.
I find them kind!
Even death
Does not dissolve and does not break
These good and tender knots,
As the sacred fire burns again in our ashes.

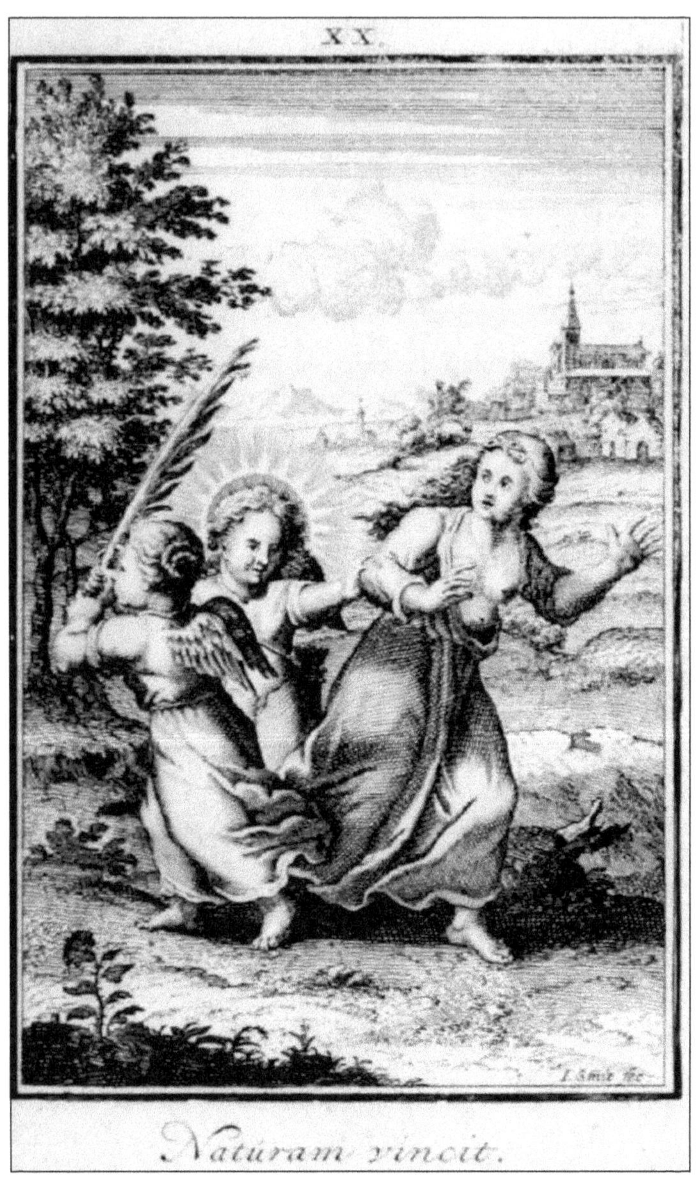

Love conquers nature

Determined, Anima now holds upright the large quill with which she had struggled with Divine Love in Emblem 12. A struggle ensues behind her, with Divine Love pushing away a tall woman symbolizing nature who looks toward Anima as if trying to get to her and possibly harm her.

Emblem 20

Love conquers nature

I am not afraid of nature
Even though we endure evil,
Since Sacred Love is my support:
Surely with him
I have the victory,
But he alone has all the glory.
He crowns my faith,
And shares with me
The fruit of his conquests;
We have thousands of victories,
And this charming conqueror,
For a reward wants only my heart.

Take, dear Love, oh take me for yourself,
Command what you love
What! Make a commandment
To love this charming Conqueror?

Ah, through this intense evil
Yet you still love!
Oh! May we live well and not be
Carried away except by the same faith,
See our Conqueror so charming
Commands our very love.

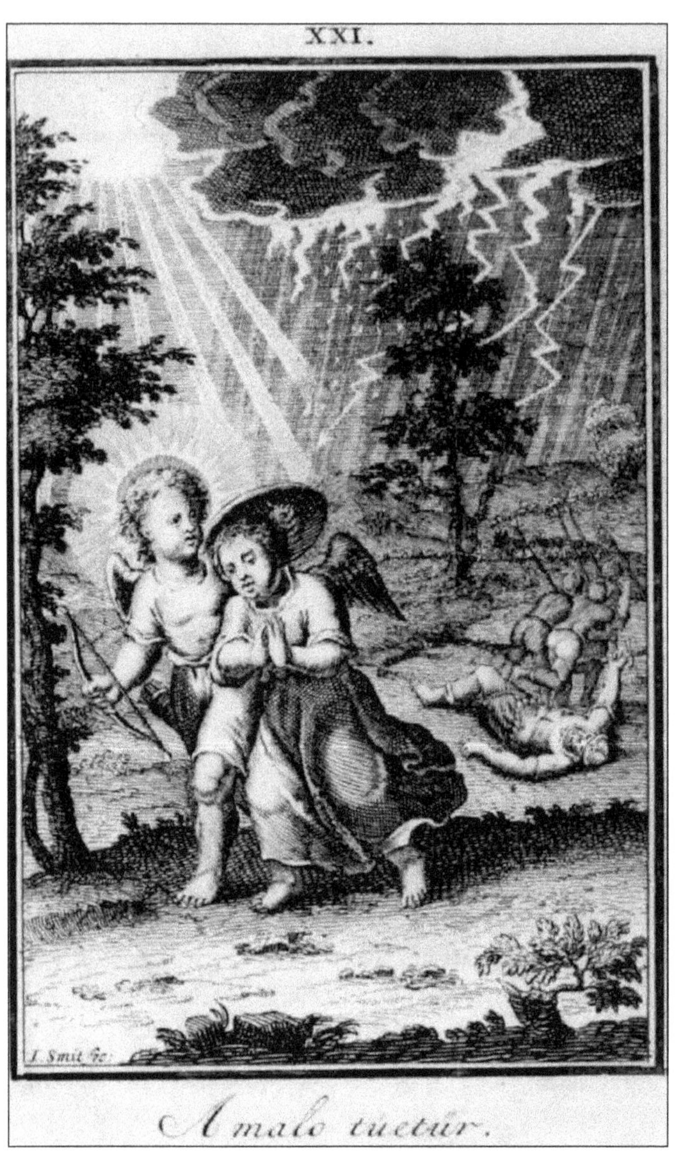

Love guards us from evil

An alert and vigilant Divine Love guides the praying Anima away from a terrifying scene where a full battle rages among soldiers with bodies scattered on the ground. Dark clouds pour forth flashing lightning and pounding rain over the darkened battle. The sun shines only on the path of Divine Love with his poised bow and arrow, as he holds a protecting shield over Anima's head.

Emblem 21

Love guards us from evil

No, no, I fear neither the winds nor storm.
With the protection of Divine Love
I feel a new courage;
Ah, how can I fear? He holds me by the hand.
He serves as my rampart; I live in assurance
Against the power of my enemies;
With such assistance
In the midst of danger, I calm my senses.

I hear the roar of floods; I see lightning strike;
I see those on my sides reduced to dust.
What do I have to fear?
I rest under the shadow of his wing,
His love fills me with strength and zeal,
For such care, he wants only my faith;
To him I abandon myself:
With no more thought, I give everything to him.

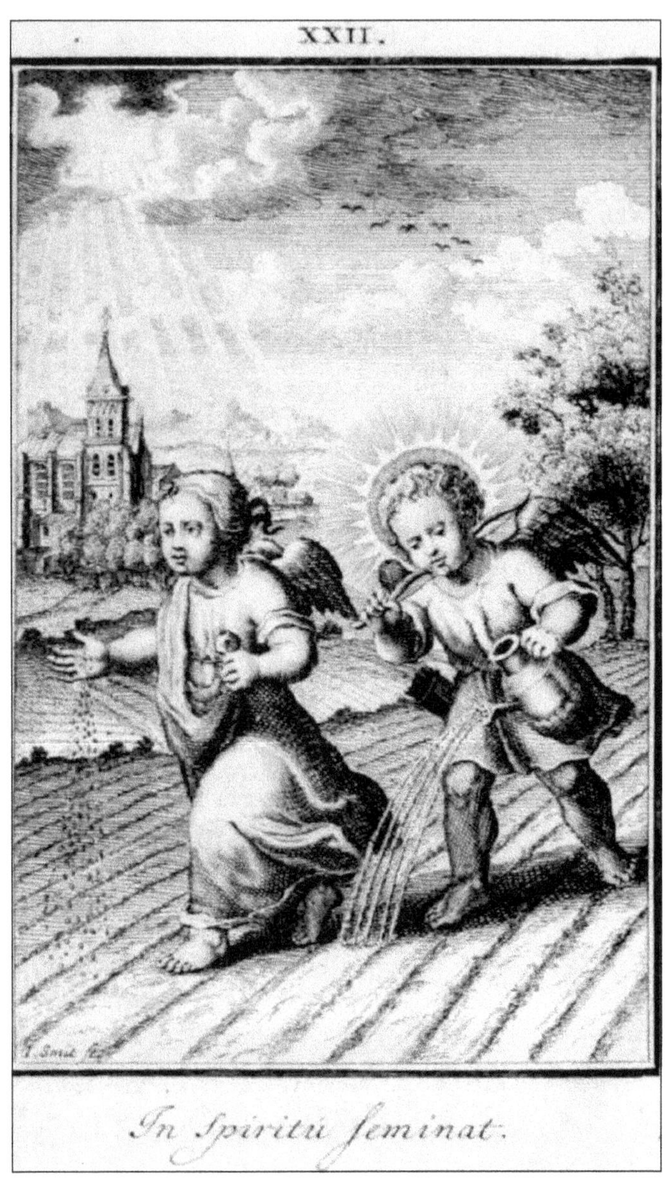

Love seeds and makes the spirit fertile

Anima and Divine Love continue their forceful, intentional walk. Now Anima leads the way, taking generous handfuls of seeds from her shoulder pouch and throwing them onto freshly plowed fields. Divine Love carefully pours water on the newly-seeded ground.

Emblem 22

Love seeds and makes the spirit fertile

O pure and holy Love,
You throw the good seed
That by divine hope
Makes eternal fruit!

Happy sown in tears!
Her labors are precious!
Rejecting weak fears,
She will be crowned in heaven.

Here a woman with pain,
Is recollected in joy a hundredfold by her labor;
Divine Love grants this to those bonded with him.
Giving thousands of honors and goods.
For her light pains and some misery.
She receives well-being.
So happy the heart that pure Love inflames!
This noble and beautiful soul
In all times and places
Lives only with her God.

Oh, what abundance
That the seed from heaven
Produces in her being!
Love pure and divine
Waters and makes grow
In this living person
Witnessed by all,
The fruits of holy Love.

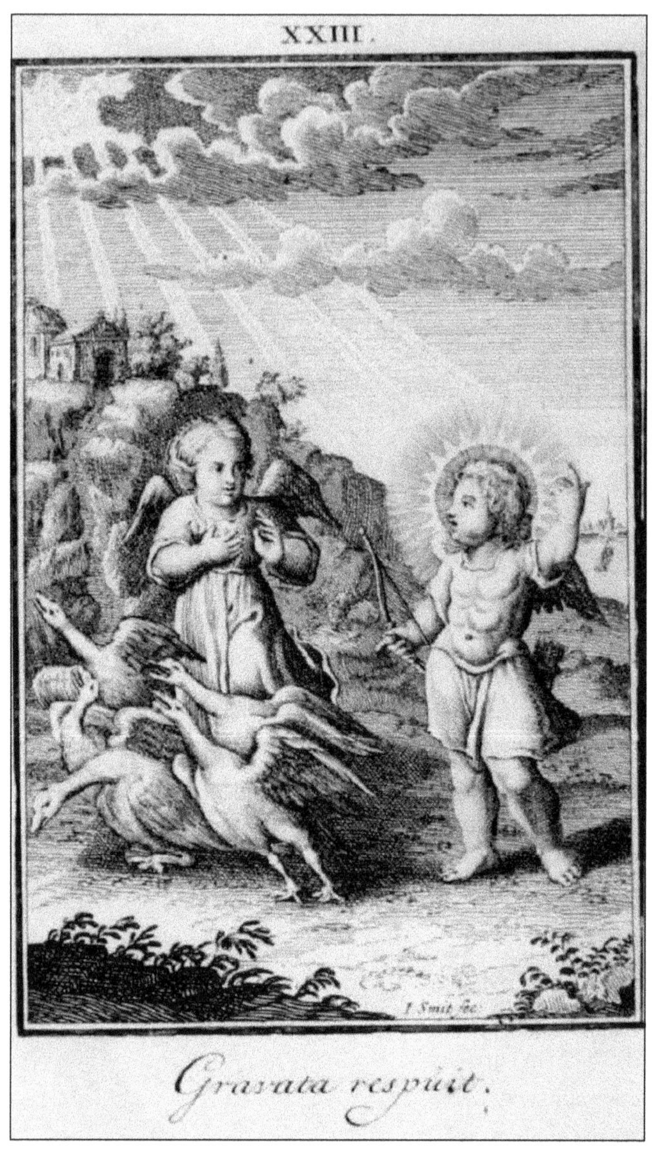

Scorning the superficial heart

Standing apart, Divine Love speaks and proclaims with an open mouth and an upraised left hand. Anima stands and attentively listens to him with her hands expressing the reception of ideas. A flock of braying geese stand in front of Anima with their small heads wildly looking in different directions while walking away from Divine Love.

Emblem 23

Scorning the superficial heart

Ah, never listen to what the flesh inspires!
Listen only to Jesus speaking to our heart:
Happy living in his kingdom!
Pleasures here below only deceive:
Those who follow them, follow a seducer.

The grace of Jesus gives strength;
Virtues serve as guides;
Divine Love, when you drive our steps
We do not become lost.

Following you, we find innocent delights.
In following the flesh, we find torments!
Sacred fire, burn me with your heavenly ardor,
Purify and burn these stains in my heart;
Rid me of contamination,
So I carry in my being an entirely pure soul.

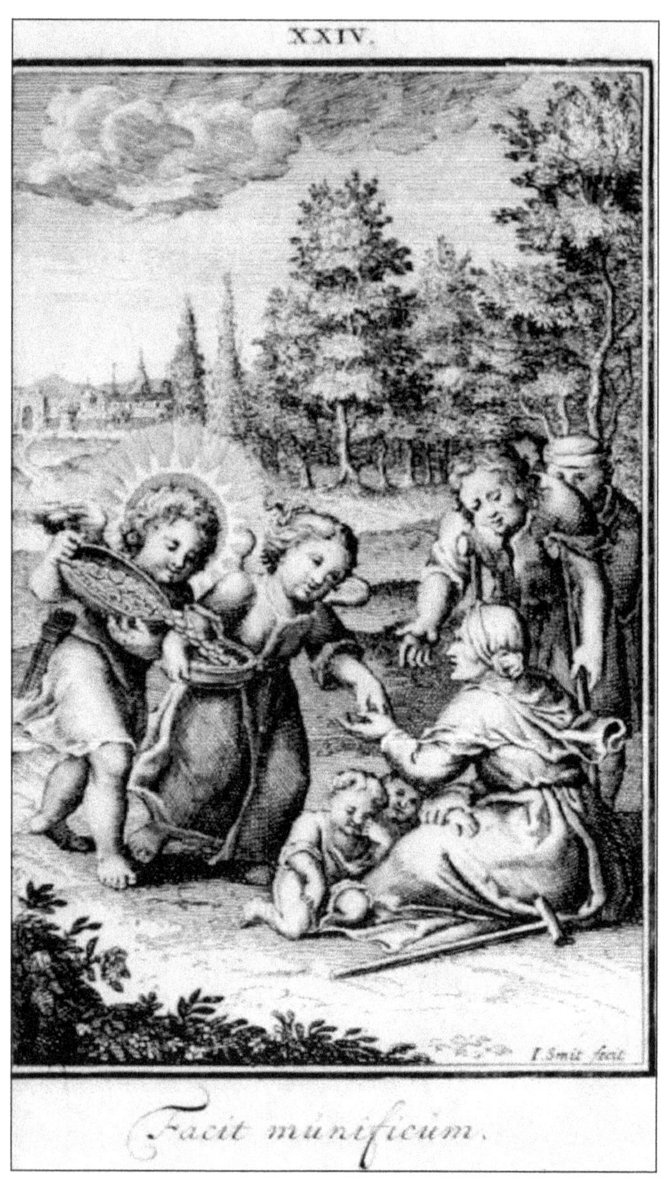

Love makes generous

With kindness Anima reaches out to give money to a poor woman sitting on the ground with two children leaning on her. Two men in need also reach out to the poor woman. As Anima hands out money, Divine Love stands behind and pours coins generously into Anima's basket.

Emblem 24

Love makes generous

How sweet it is when we give without receiving!
The more I give, the more you press on me
And I receive new gifts.
Your riches are immense,
Divine Love, gifts so beautiful
You increase our rewards.

Lord, you reward me with gifts,
You crown me with merit:
If I serve you and please you,
If I accomplish my duty,
Is it not only that I want your kindness?

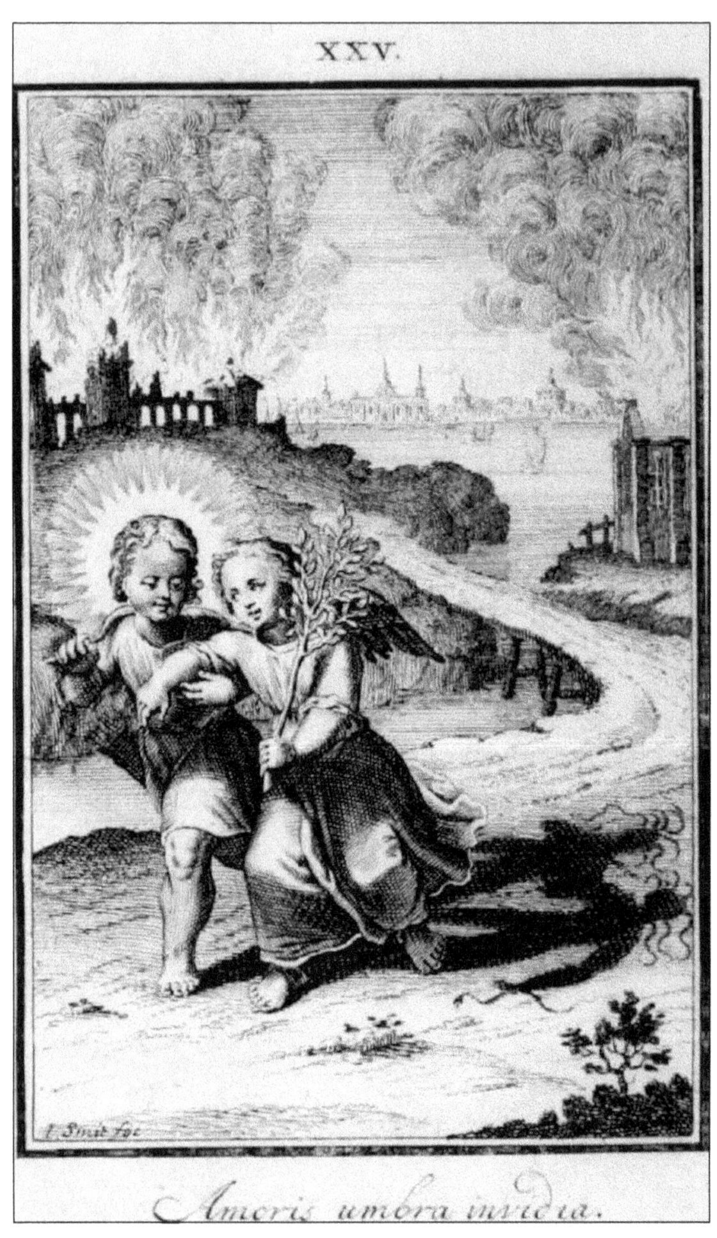

Jealousy is the shadow of Love

Anima leans on Divine Love's arm as he guides her away from burning cities engulfed by flames. Behind them, cities burn on one side of an ocean bay and on the other side peaceful cities rest secure.

Emblem 25

Jealousy is the shadow of Love

I love you, O my God, much more than my life,
And I always want to love you:
Yet others envy me,
But your gentle hand disarms all of them.

When your divine fire took hold of my heart,
When I felt the burn of your favorable flame
Consuming my soul,
I immediately noticed the jealous fury
Following me as the shadow follows the fire.
And when you appear,
I suddenly see you
In all times and places.

As soon as Pure Love wants to serve as a guide,
From the moment he commands us,
The jealous destruction follows,
We feel its blows.

My Jesus, your grace
Will be my support.
I understand nothing except
You are my way and your fire is my delight.

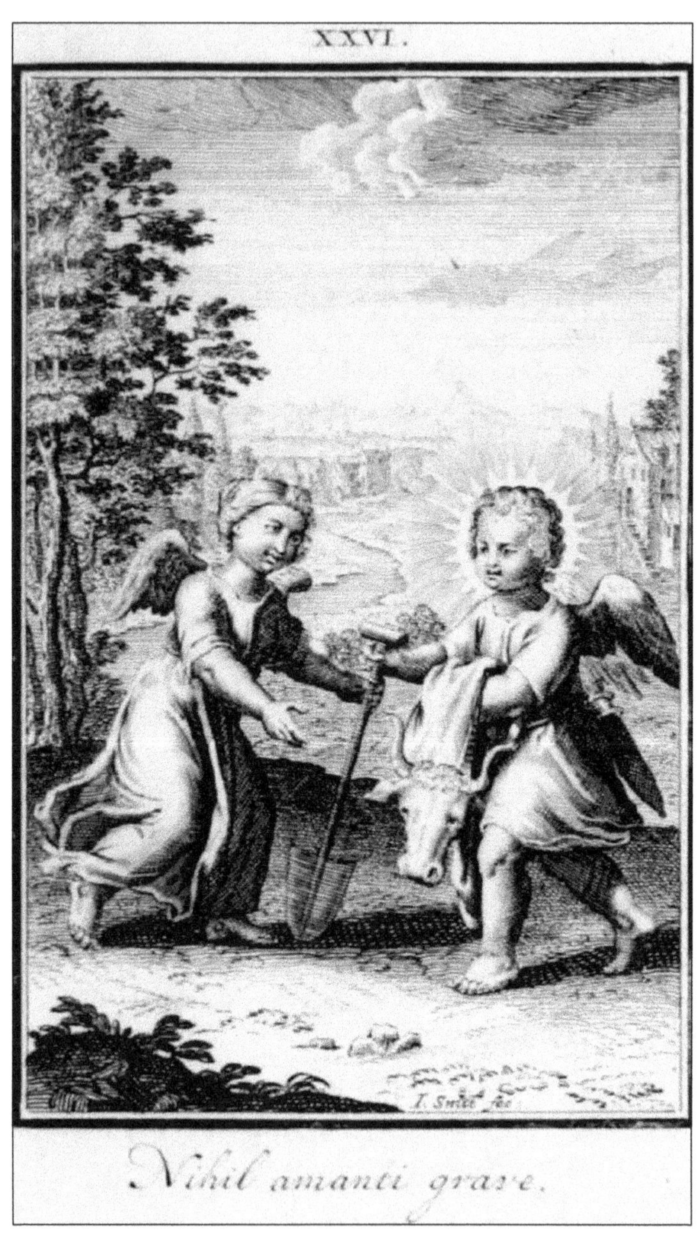

Nothing weighs on one who loves

Both Anima and Divine Love have their hands on a shovel in the dirt. Divine Love carries an ox head with the empty skin draped over his arm.

Emblem 26

Nothing weighs on one who loves

When we love God with a true love,
The most difficult work appears light.
The yoke of our Lord is sweet!
To please him we fear neither torments nor dangers.

Perfect love cannot fear punishment,
Who fears loves feebly:
Who fears the yoke and the chain,
Is not a true lover.
Suffering for what you love
Is a charming pleasure
When love is intense.

Love, your divine rigor pleases,
Nothing is as good or kind:
In truth a good heart
Is preferred
To all other sweetness!

Sweet and pleasant work!
Delicious load
Expanding my soul
You please my heart though contrary to sense!
Ah, that my martyrdom
Never ends, Love, until I die!

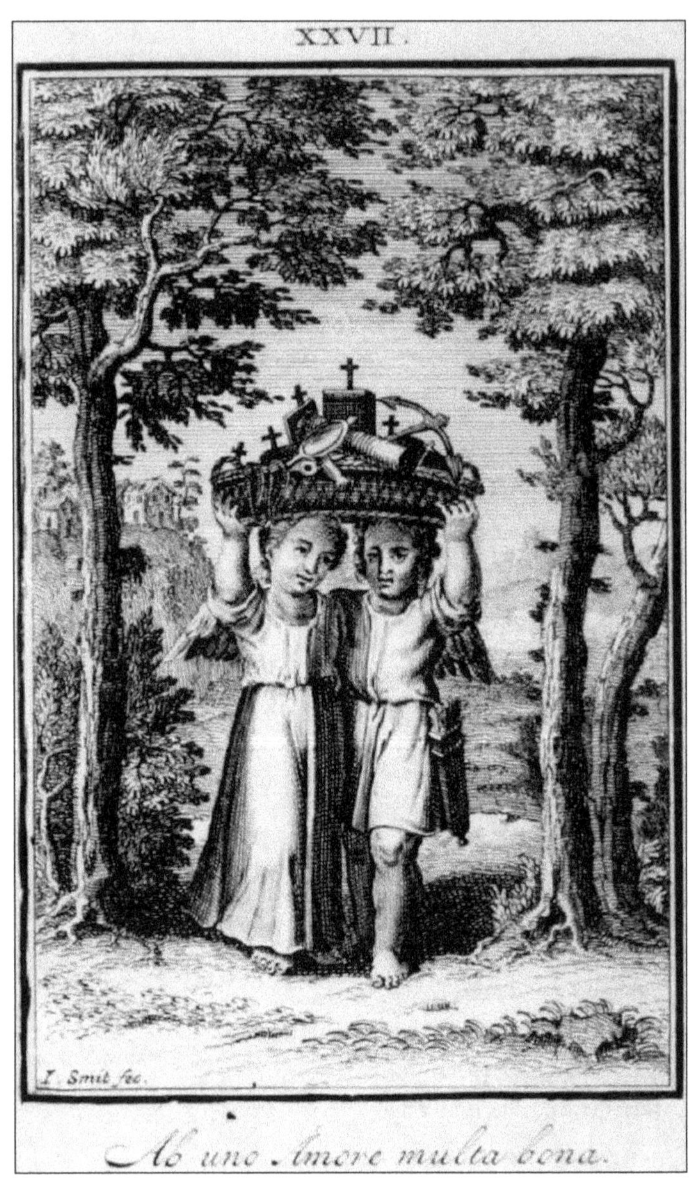

Only Love is the source of good

Looking more like twins now, Anima and Divine Love stand tall in the midst of erect and straight trees. They jointly carry a basket on their heads that looks like a hat. In the basket are many different sizes and shapes of crosses along with a large anchor and other tools.

Emblem 27

Only Love is the source of good

In union with Love, we find all that is good.
Love communicates life
In this sweet place
Where the soul is bonded.
These happy lovers
Taste deep contentment.

Of all of the virtues, pure Love crowns;
Far from being burdened by this weight,
We know this as a favor given to us
And experience immediate relief.
A divine assembly,
O happiness without parallel!
Dear and sweet togetherness
Agreeable apparel!

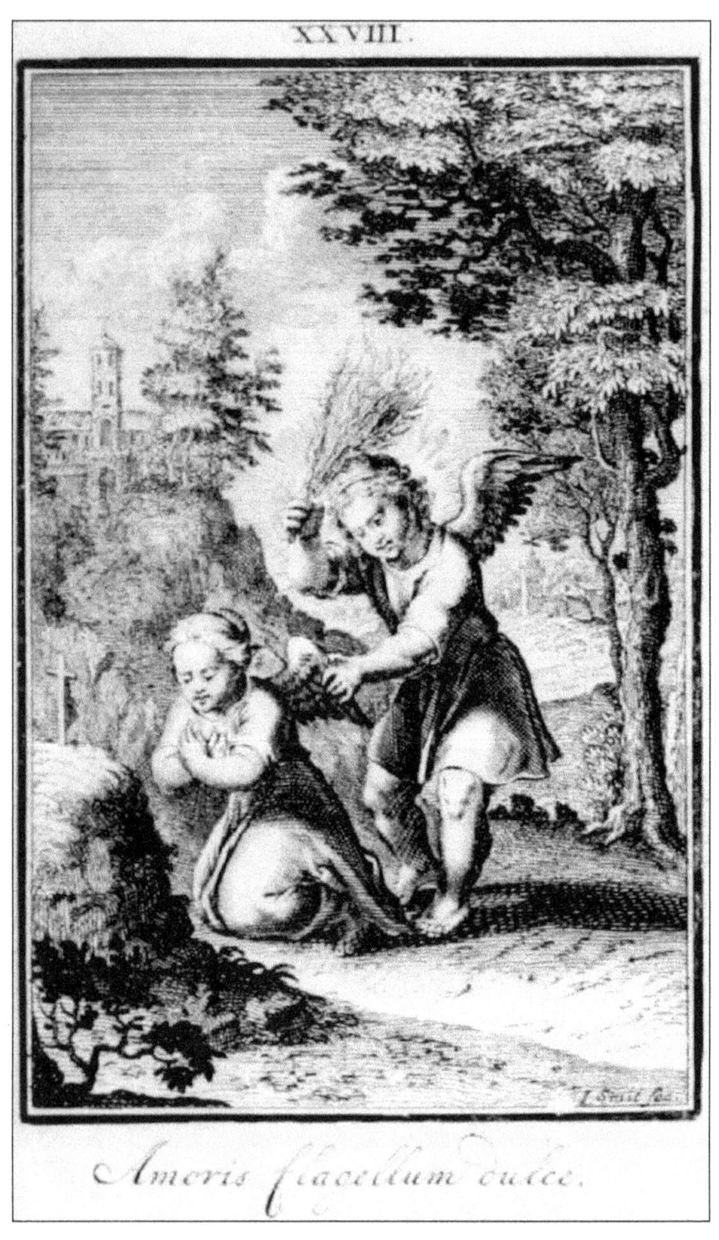

The blows of Love are sweet

Anima kneels in prayer facing toward a cross and away from Divine Love while he holds over her back a branch of leaves. Both Divine Love and Anima are smiling.

Emblem 28

The blows of Love are sweet

Love, what should I do?
I see you are angry:
Ah, I fear not, Love, your wrath:
I fear your absence, not your blows.
Any coldness from you
Is harder than any vengeance.

Open my heart, but do not be angry:
I adore your laws and find a thousand charms
Even in your justice,
I am with you step by step.

Always for you, I challenge myself,
I cherish the fruitfulness of your intense love,
And find them charming:
Do not spare me, my adorable Father,
If you are not angry with me,
I am most contented.

But if you do get angry, I can no longer live;
Bring together all your fire,
Make me the most unfortunate,
But always let me follow you.

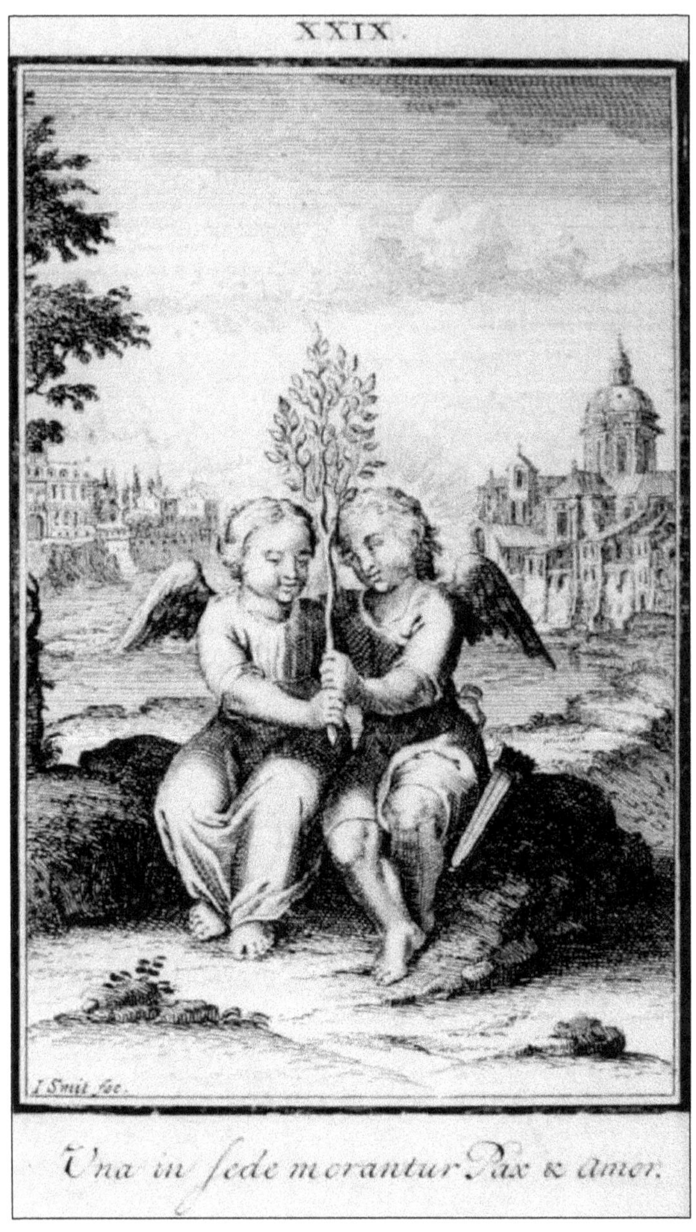

Peace and love abide together

Anima and Love sit directly next to each other jointly holding the branch of leaves over their head. All appears sweet and peaceful.

Emblem 29

Peace and love abide together

Calm and tranquility always
Accompany pure and sincere love;
Sweet peace necessarily
Discerns holy charity in us.
Trouble and chagrin always accompany
The lack of love, whether in the city or the country.
In pleasure or sadness,
Equanimity is our happiness:
Peace follows and brings delights
Even in the midst of difficulties.

You promised well, O my divine Bridegroom,
This peace only proceeds from you;
This peace surpasses all things,
And produces your grace in me,
Which the world cannot give,
Peace that we do not understand:
O my great God, I love and adore you,
With all my heart, I want to abandon myself to you.

Your peace is my wealth,
My zeal and my fortress:
Filling my heart with you.
Peace is; You are:
Let us be silent in the throes of creation.
Taste peace, my heart; language, stay quiet;
And never end
This happy peace!

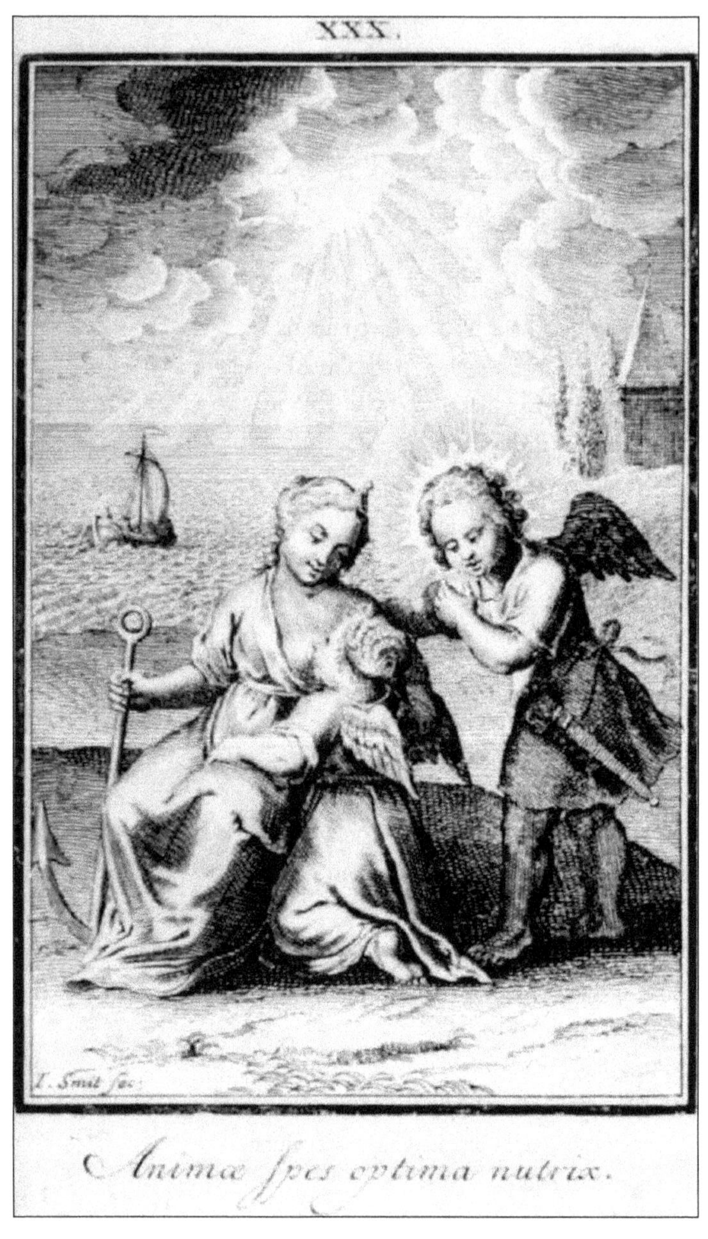

Hope nourishes the lover's soul

On a sandy beach, Anima kneels before a queen representing hope. Divine Love, Hope, and Anima communes with each other.

Emblem 30

Hope nourishes the lover's soul

Hope serves food to the true lover
In the work that we endure:
Pure charity and sincere faith
In holiness rule life.
The soul whom God ravishes
Finds nothing except
This unique Good.
God alone contents and brings pleasure,
Peace touching and filling our desire.

Happy hope!
Since in advance, one receives
In confident expectation, his promised happiness
A constant soul, nourished spirit,
A fervent love with unfeigned faith,
Contentment reigns, pure and whole.

With great courage the generous heart
Sees thunderstorms melt away:
The frothy waves disappear
Before its very eyes.
The committed heart is not touched,
Her eyes see the very Lord:
The soul rests in his sacred heart.

Admirable lover,
You live content
Despite the dangers!
Your evils are light,
The good is immense,
Your heart without worry.
Who is this?
This is your hope.

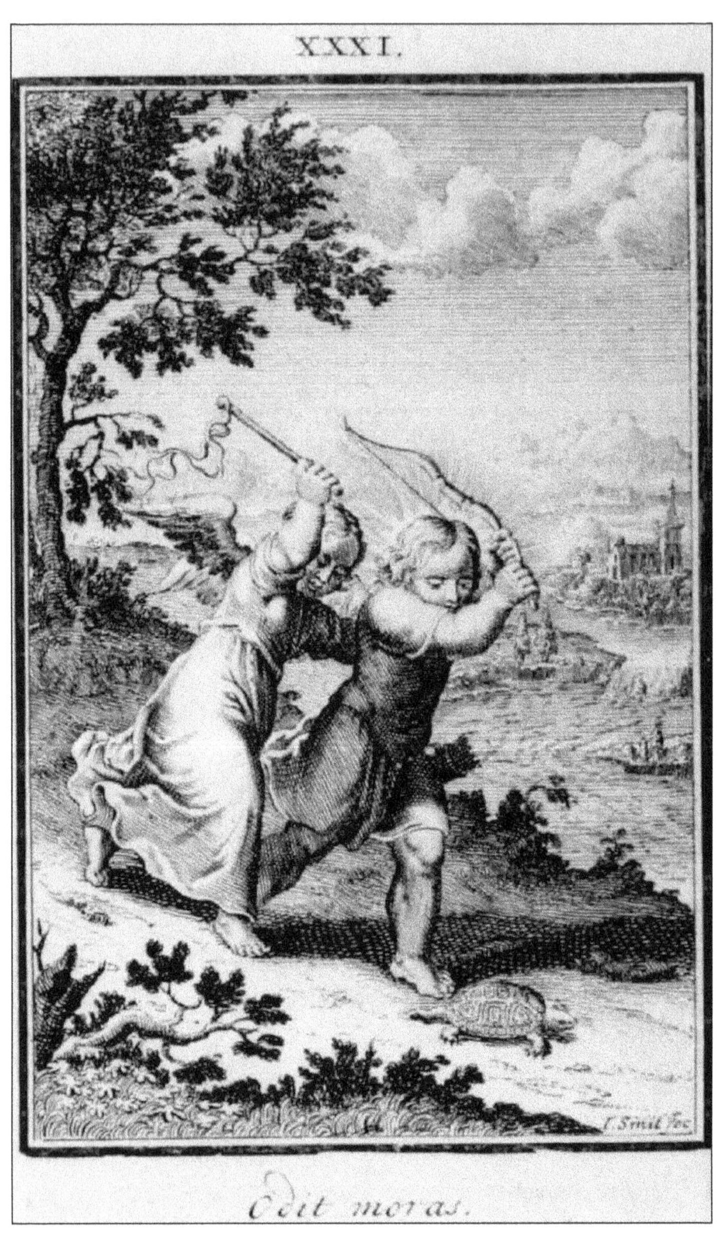

Love hates delays

Anima with a raised stick and Divine Love with a raised bow chase a large, slow turtle down a winding, dirt path.

Emblem 31

Love hates delays

Divine Love hates all nonchalance,
As soon as it takes a heart
He gives it a holy vigor
Opposed to negligence.

As soon as we love goodness, we become diligent,
Love makes the soul always alert;
We watch and pray fervently,
To our powerful God.
We do not complain when undergoing suffering,
We grow through the sufferings
Because it is right to die to ourselves;
In faith, Love holds all rewards.

Pure love is different
Than slow indolence!
The faithful lover advances eagerly
To the way of Providence:
Always ready to go, content with everything,
Whatever happens, and whatever it undertakes
It arrives surely at the end
Aided by the sovereign hand.

When Jesus leads our steps,
Who does not run, who does not fly?
We have no fear of precipices,
In his work, we find delights;
Finally, we run constantly,
After all, the repose lasts through eternity.

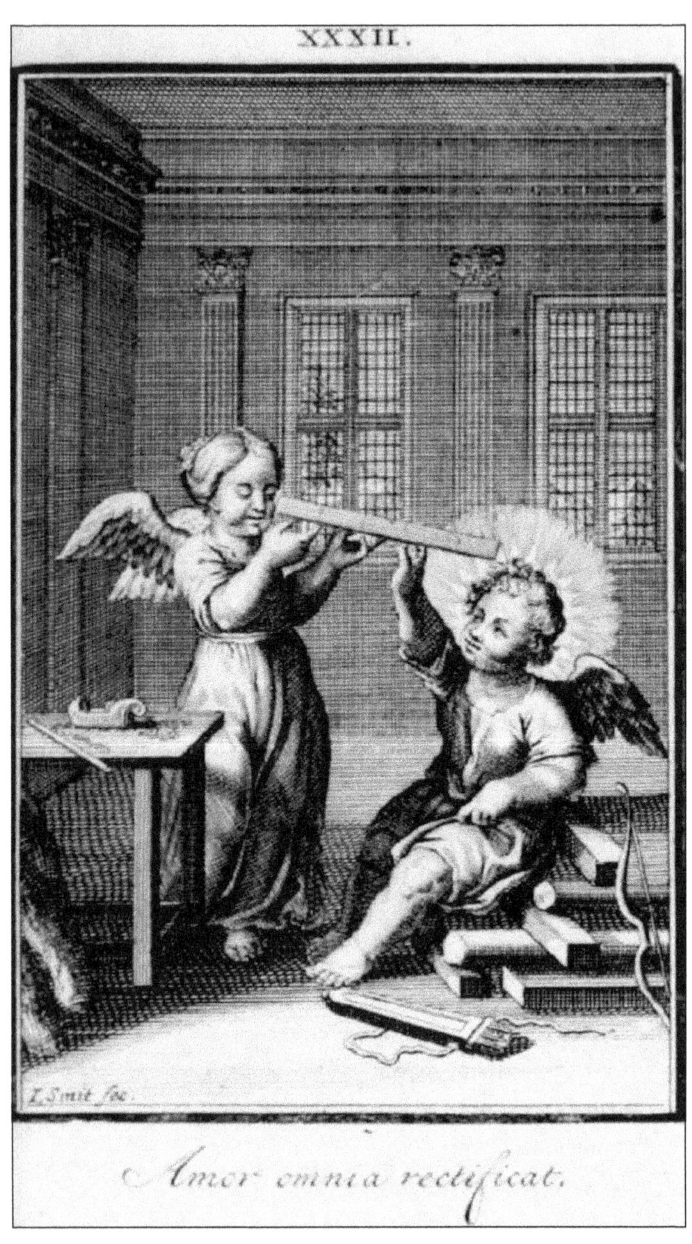

Love makes everything right

Divine Love and Anima hold opposite ends of a measuring tool. They are working together on a project with wood, materials, and tools scattered around them.

Emblem 32

Love makes everything right

Love corrects and rules
Any faults in our conduct;
Nothing can equal
The goodness of a pure soul instructed by Love.

A heart that follows Love's song
Has no lies or error.
Pure Love teaches his lovers
Righteousness and peace with
Solid humility.
They prevent detours and vanity;
Candor, sincerity,
Good faith, joy, and innocence,
Are sound science.
"If you are," says he, "like children
You can please me:
You love me and satisfy me,
I delight in your heart,
And I give you happiness.

"It is not the sages of the world
To whom I reveal my secrets:
It is the small children with profound humility
Who penetrate my holy decrees.
The small ones who are kind
With sweetness and attractions!
The others have a hateful finesse
With detours, mazes, and nets.
With them, he who deceives best passes for the wisest;
For their next move, they take advantage,
They pass for clever and witty.
Yet who are the most contented: my children or them?"

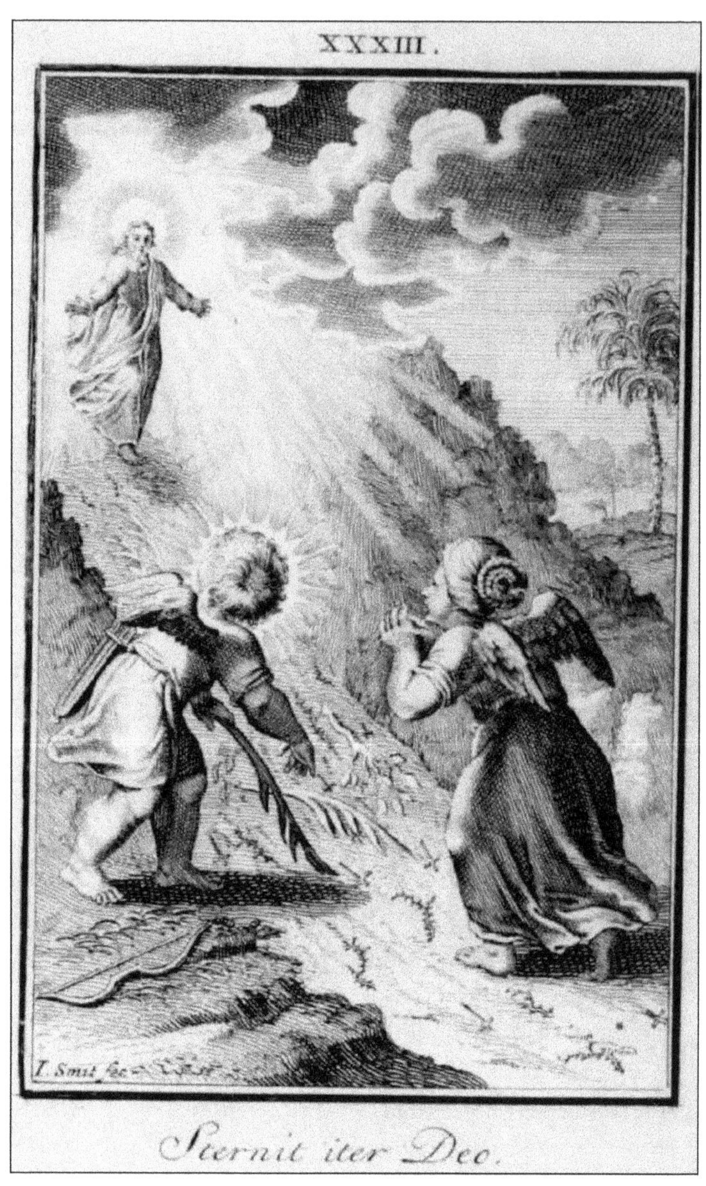

Love prepares the way to God

God the Father appears at the top of an upward path. God appears as a transcendent and mysterious figure with outstretched hands, surrounded by light. The riveted Anima waits at the bottom of the path covered with palm branches and thorns. Divine Love has his face entirely turned to the revealed God.

Emblem 33

Love prepares the way to God

Jesus is the Way, the Truth, and the Life;
Follow him to find the path and the place.
Despite the demons and their mortal envy,
We are surely led and guided to God.

Whoever follows Jesus walks in his light,
He has a torch in the darkest night,
He makes our heart all full of grace
As he leads, he assures, and instructs.

Although this beautiful way appears full of thorns,
Yet it is easy and full of flowers:
How sweet it is to walk in the divine way!
Our own hearts and spirits are misleading guides.

O my Jesus, without you I cannot follow,
Give me your hand and conduct my steps:
Your divine hand delivers me out of traps:
With your support, I will not tremble.

When following you, I do not fear abysses and precipices:
I love you so much,
By enduring for you the most frightful torments
I lose without sorrow the light of day.

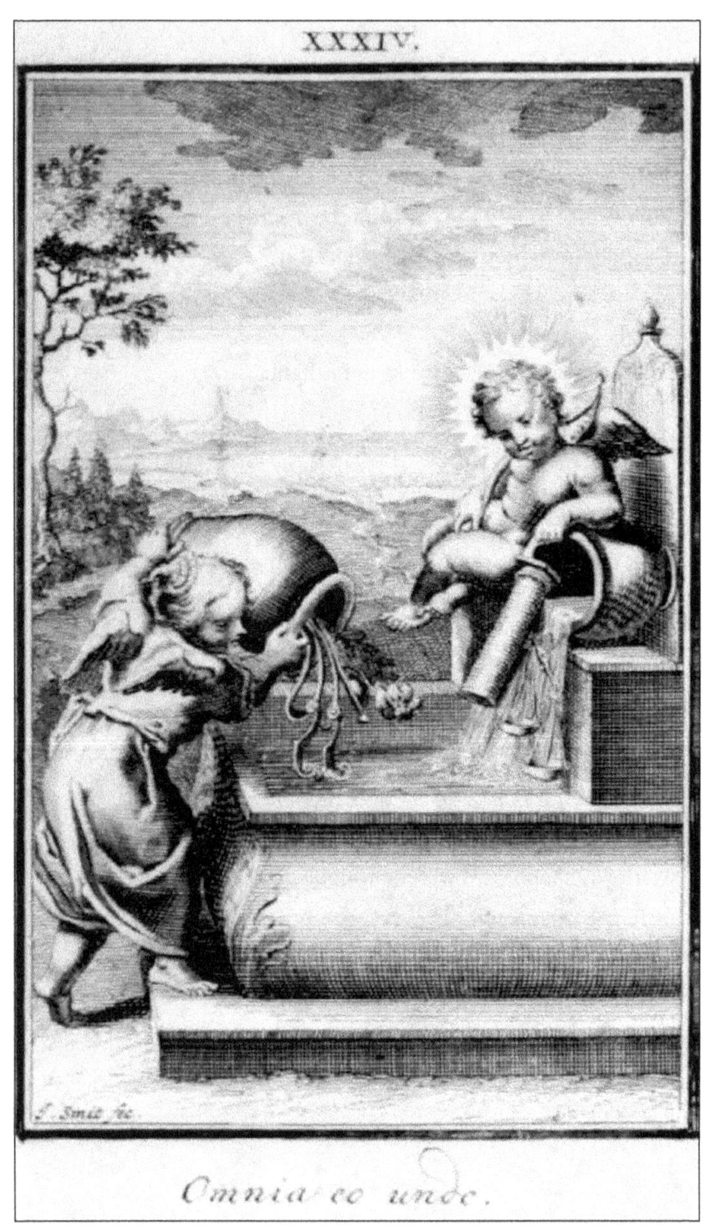

Everything must return to its first source

Divine Love sits pouring water from a vase into a fountain. Along with the water, other objects, such as scales and a telescope, tumble out. At a lower level Anima also pours water and symbolic objects from a vase.

Emblem 34

Everything must return to its first source

Your generosity,
Love, is magnificent and grand;
Its noble and beautiful quality
Is what I ask of you!
But when you give, you want a return;
Permit me this word, Divine Love,
Some interest, it seems, motivates you;
You give the virtues and want fruits:
But may we refuse you without crime,
Since you by your Love produced these?

Virtue without love is a barren tree;
Love makes all fertile:
Divine love differs
From the one we see in the world,
Whose heat so far from being fruitful
Destroys, consumes, and reproduces nothing.
Sacred fire in our heart
Gives birth.
The good seed through heavenly passion
Grows and flourishes.

O fire divine, producing all things,
You carry us
Into eternal happiness.
What hope, abundance, and sweetness!
Innocent delights, O happy rigor,
O holy Love, you will be our eternal home!

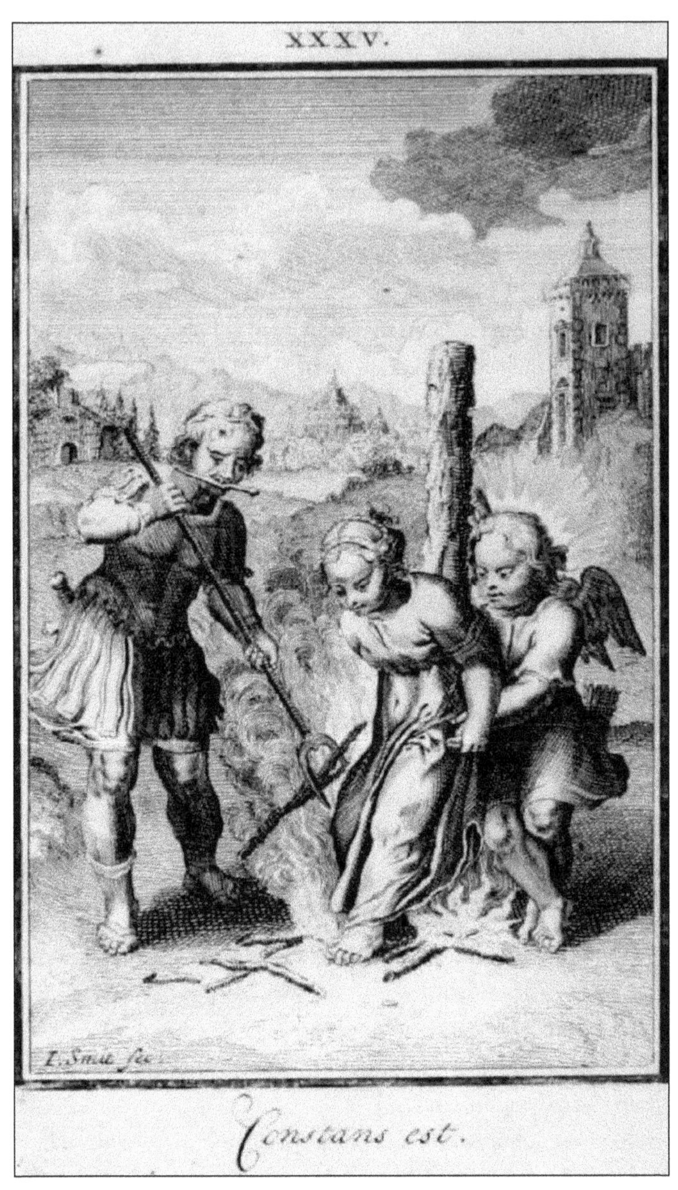

Love is firm and constant

Divine Love ties Anima to a tree trunk where she will suffer martyrdom. Carrying a long nail in his mouth, the torturer has begun the flames and is heating up a rod in the fire. With flames already licking at Anima's feet, she looks at several crosses made of the torturer's tools on the ground.

Emblem 35

Love is firm and constant

Love, with you the harshest torments
Pass for contentment;
Torture and fire, test my constancy:
Born of your power,
This unique assistance brings
Infinite happiness. Your presence
Takes away the feeling of this most terrible punishment;
The executioner's weapons begin and
Yet I have much more than horror and
Excessive pain.

Love, the source of my delight,
Abandon me not in the midst of torture:
If you abandon me, alas!
Love, do I fear?
Sustained by your powerful hand
My soul easily remains constant!

Ah, that I should soon be overwhelmed,
I would be weak and fearful
If you abandoned me for a moment to myself!
When you support me by your supreme grace,
I know more. I am victorious against
These enemies' fury:
Even if I fall in appearance
Your power explodes before their very eyes.

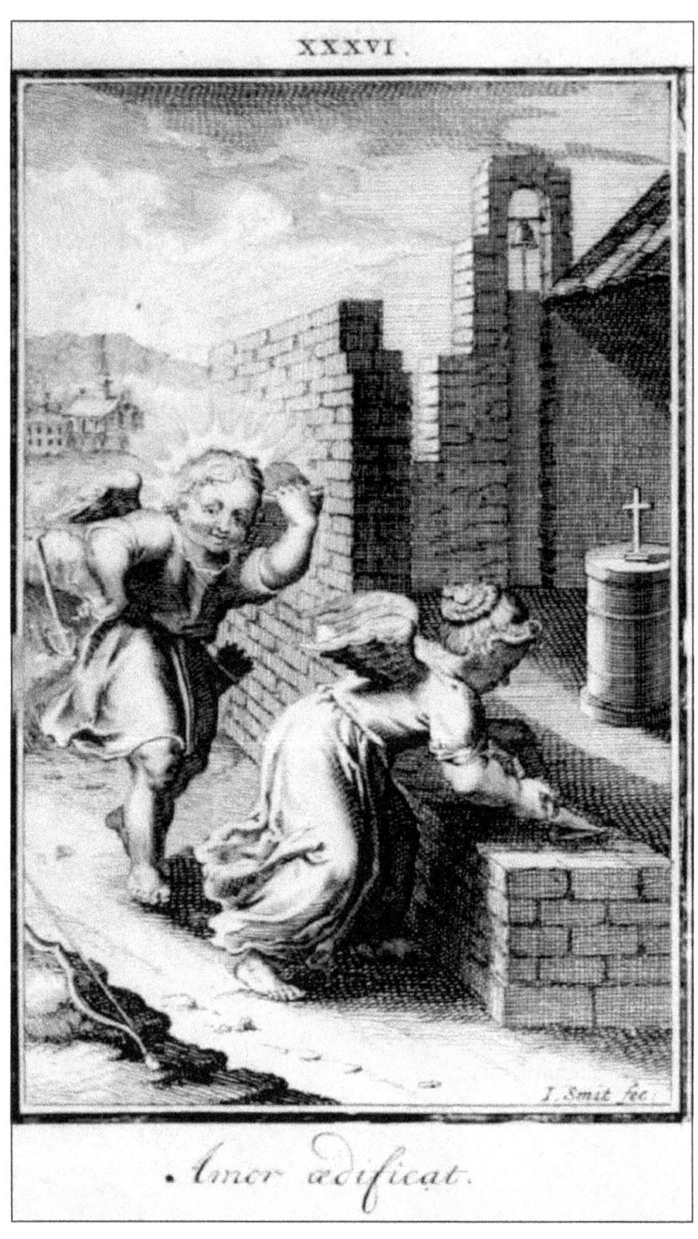

Love edifies and builds

Industriously Anima builds a sturdy brick building around a circular pedestal with a cross on top. Divine Love carries her materials on his back. The large building has a tower with a bell on one high wall.

Emblem 36

Love edifies and builds

O Divine Love is a good architect!
You build in our hearts a pleasant home
Dedicated to Love.
Where we serve, love, and respect.

In the bottom of my heart, God makes his home,
He founds, builds, adorns, and beautifies it.
God dwells there eternally.
He engraves and polishes our home.

God cares, offering everything.
Oh, I am happy when with eyes of faith,
I contemplate the sovereign Goodness.
I die perfectly in order to live for the divine King!
Revived by the Spirit's spring, I see in faith
The living water discovered by the Samaritan woman.
Yes, as an interior human
I find in my heart this living fountain.
In truth I adore the Father;
His eternal Spirit grounds the earth.

Take, O my God, my heart as your temple:
Despite all storms and noise,
I have the quiet of your night,
When in power I contemplate you.

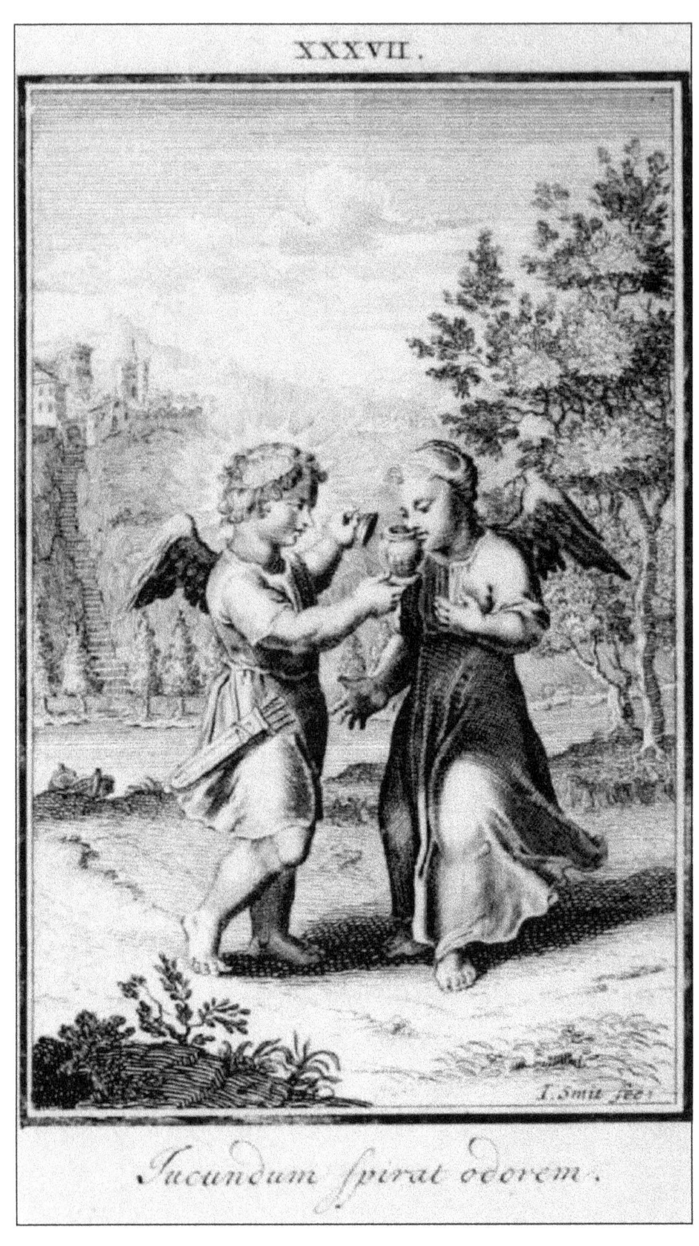

Love breathes a charming fragrance

Divine Love holds a chalice filled with fragrances to Anima's face for her to smell. With a regal look, Divine Love wears a crown and far off behind them, a long, steep staircase leads to a gracious village.

Emblem 37

Love breathes a charming fragrance

Draw me, my God, my only hope,
By your precious perfume:
Already I feel myself fainting,
Because this delicious balm,
Strengthens my heart and gives me courage,
I will run after you to any place:
I do not desire to have any other portion
On earth or in heaven.

Withdraw your sweetness, pleasures, favors, caresses;
O God, it is you only that I want,
You are my all, my strength, my riches,
Only you can make me happy.

I sense that your perfume is a wonderful power,
I discern the aroma:
O divine Bridegroom, whom I adore and love,
You alone fulfill my heart.

For a moment you take away the delightful taste
And sight of you,
These are rigorous torments.
Then everything is bitter for me,
You only are sweet,
You only are kind,
You only fill my desires.
Without you is anything delightful?
In you are enclosed trustworthy pleasures.

Since you fulfill yourself, my Lord,
Can you fulfill me?
You unite your kindness with supreme grandeur:
Who misses your charms?

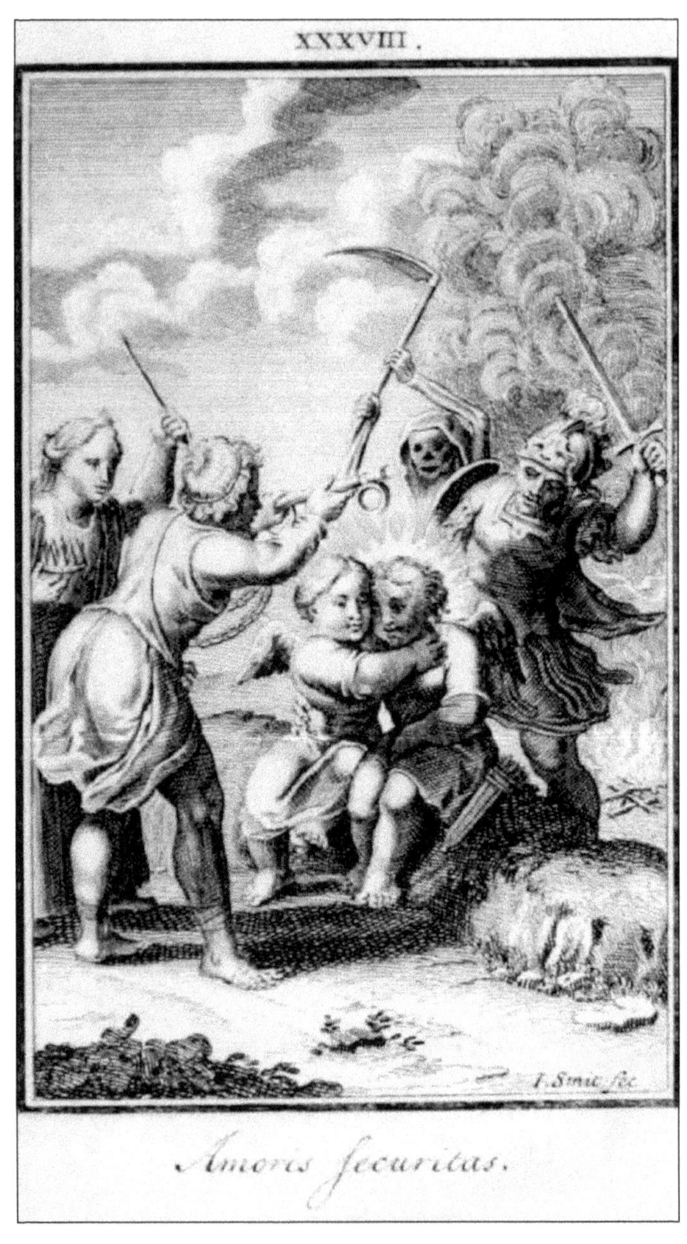

Love makes us secure

Intimately Divine Love and Anima sit next to each other embracing, yet now an angry mob surrounds them brandishing swords and weapons ready to strike them. Over the shoulders of the mob leers the skeleton face of death's Grim Reaper.

Emblem 38

Love makes us secure

I laugh at the executioner's efforts!
I do not fear death,
Near to my Beloved, I am safe:
You make me defiant:
Approach with your chains and irons,
I have contempt for your various torments.

When Divine Love takes over our soul,
And we feel his favorable flame,
That consumes in us all propriety,
We disengage from the self and live in freedom.
Chains, prisons, do not cause us fear,
The sword can never reach us.

Are we frightened at the horror of death?
Death brings to my heart a thousand secret charms:
It may take off my fragile life,
Yet a sovereign happiness follows this loss,
Since I infallibly fall
Into the arms of my Lover.
Ah, are we afraid to see what we love?
Whatever Love costs,
I find the price too low
To enjoy forever the divine charms.

When Love seizes our heart,
Hunger, nakedness, nothing can separate us,
Death, hell, persecution,
Nothing can prevent this holy union.

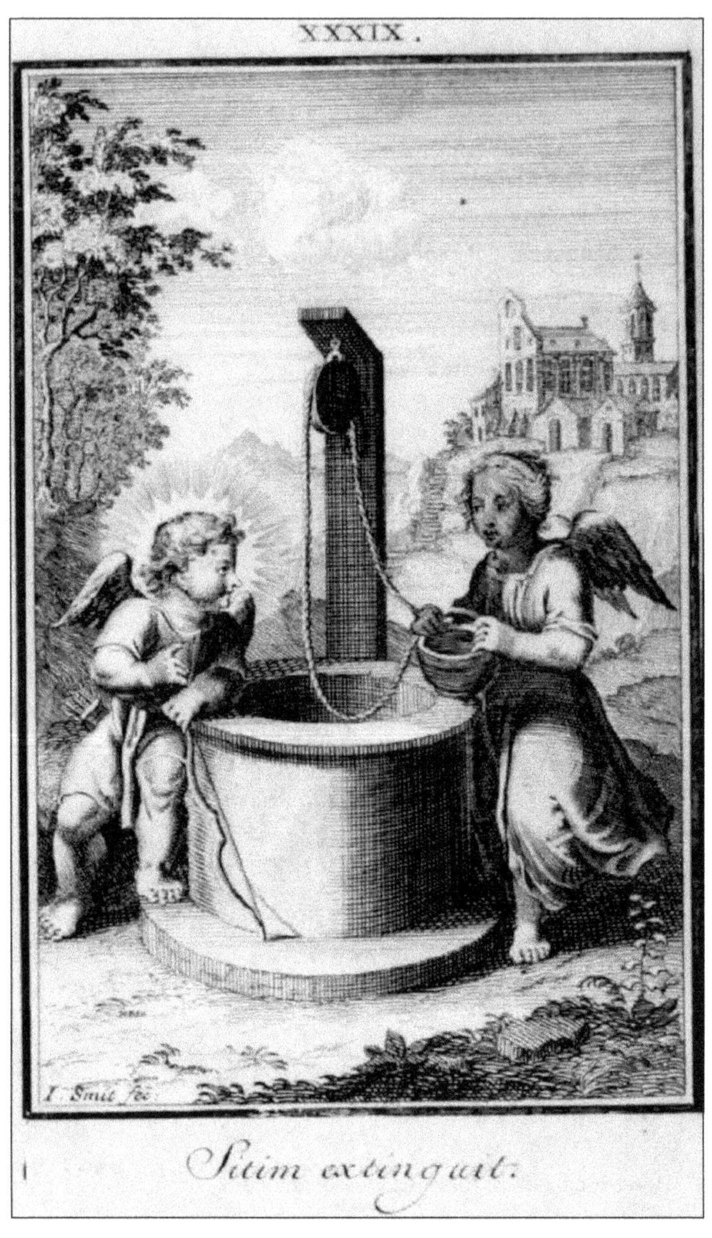

Love quenches the thirst of the heart

In serenity Divine Love leans against a country well while Anima, standing in a shadow on the other side, prepares to put her bucket down for water. Anima's face now looks developed and beautiful.

Emblem 39

Love quenches the thirst of the heart

Delights of the spirit, I prefer you
Over the false pleasures of the senses.
They are only apparent; you are real.
They disappoint; you solidly satisfy.

Divine Truth, who the world ignores,
You fill my heart with celestial ardor.
Source of all my good, dear Bridegroom whom I adore,
Your healing waters flow in my heart.
That sacred river flows into my soul
These prominent waters of Divinity
Extinguish in me any flame except
The love of your Truth.
The water makes it more ardent, pure, and luminous.
Love burns brightly.

Give me this water that maintains life;
For its lack causes death;
This body holds me enslaved and
Hinders my efforts.

My soul is stronger than my body:
You, my Lord, break these bonds,
Ah, let my body return to dust
Give my spirit the true good!

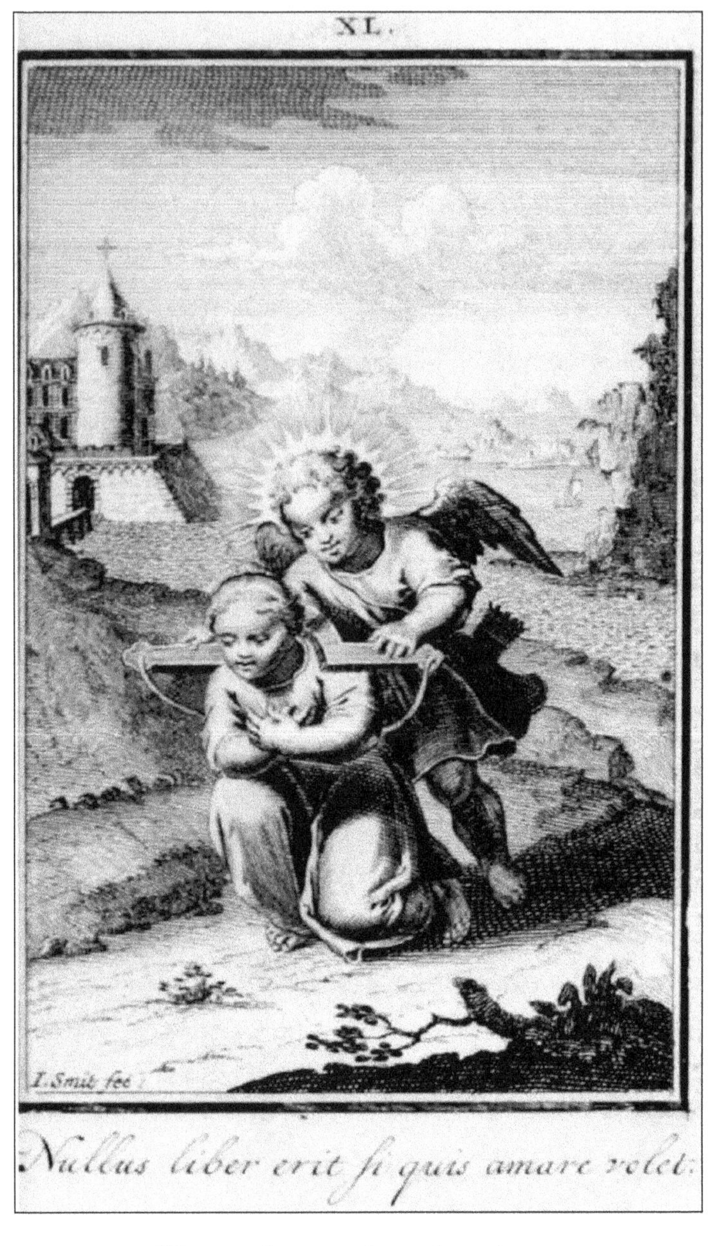

Who wants Love is not free to choose the way

Tenderly Divine Love places a large wooden cross on Anima's back. As she kneels, Anima prays in a dirt road that leads up a hill.

Emblem 40

Who wants Love is not free to choose the way

I love your gentle and sweet yoke,
I fear vanity!
I am free and far from slavery,
When I carry you in love.

My soul is happy to be your captive!
I find here my liberty.
Love, let me live
In humble dependence on your will.

Happy yoke that ends my captivity,
And causes a vast delight.
This brings harmony with the sweet flame
I keep in my heart as a precious gift.

The world sees only the apparent load
Thinking I am overwhelmed,
And believes I am very unfortunate: but my wide heart,
Far from being a slave, is filled with delights.

No, the world can hardly comprehend
That happiness lies within;
The world loves that which destroys:
Flattering honors and sensory pleasures.

The children of Jesus are far more wise,
By desiring nothing and enjoying the cross:
Ah, the taste of a delicacy,
The favor of a good choice!

I give away society, worldly honors, delights;
I love my work, my chains, my prison:
When I suffer all these torments,
I find again that I have great purpose:
Say without artifice,
The One who knows Love and the just valor,
And who returns justice,
Approves the traits of my heart.

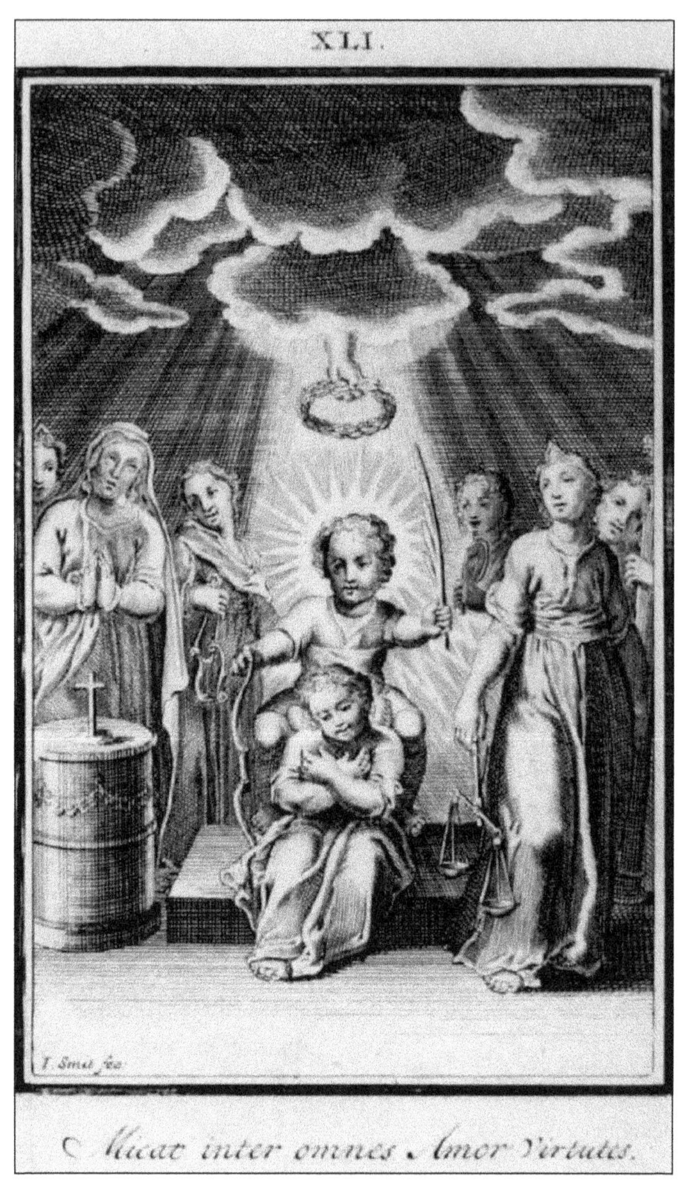

Unique love shines among all the virtues

With the six virtues in the background, humble Anima sits on a low platform and Divine Love, standing tall behind her, holds a guide rope that goes between them. A hand reaches down from the clouds of heaven with a crown and at the side rests a circular altar with a simple cross on top.

Emblem 41

Unique love shines among all the virtues

Divine Love with understanding
Brings supreme excellence to all the virtues.
Source of justice and sustenance of faith,
You hold everything we hope.

Without you penitence is hypocrisy,
Prudence and power is pure mania;
Without you, Divine Love, the cross, martyrdom, torments,
Are only vain amusements.

Sacred Love rules all things;
Love is our goal
Giving us the good, strength, and courage,
All languishes without Love's noble vigor,
Flying to heaven while clinging to earth,
Love lives in our hearts amidst both peace and war;
Always through Love we are victorious:
It straightens our steps and opens our eyes.

All is misery without its sweet assistance!
Our only hope in work,
Our only appeal in afflictions.
Sacred Love, govern and conduct my days
By order of your providence;
I want to live and die dependent on you!

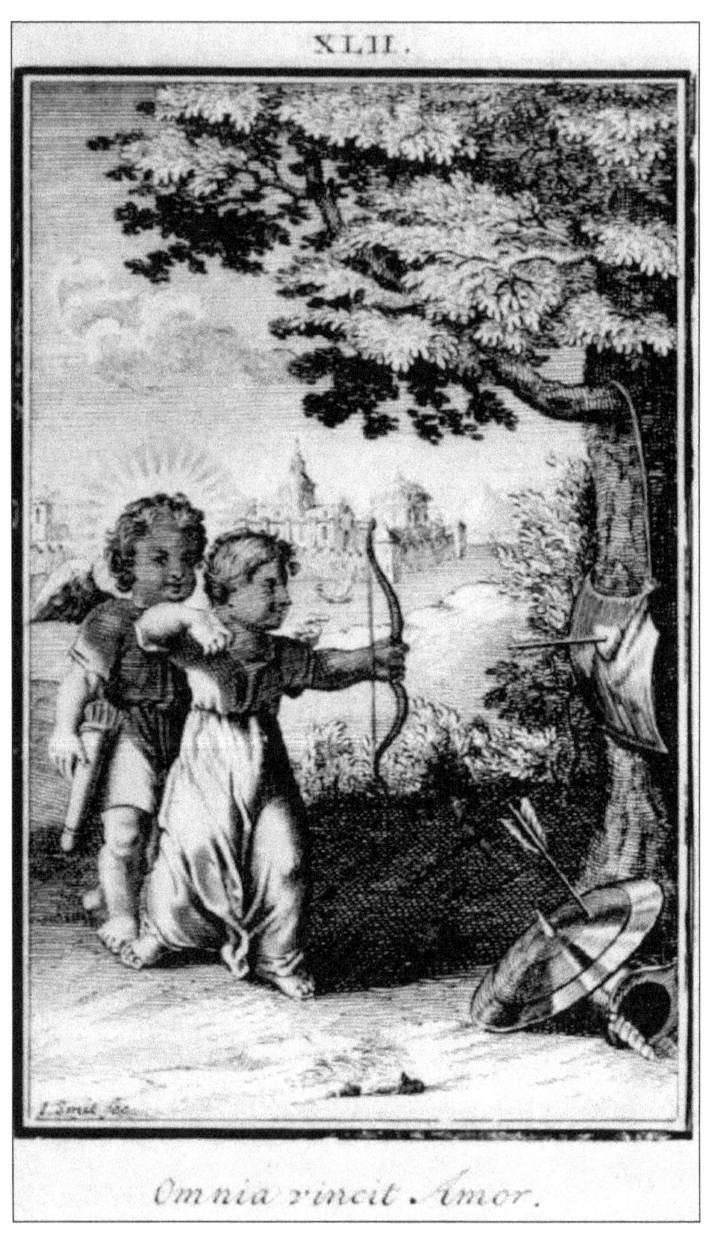

Love overcomes all

Divine Love stands behind an energetic and forceful Anima who aims her arrow and shoots at her heart pinned to a tree. A shield with an arrow in it lies at the foot of the tree.

Emblem 42

Love overcomes all

Who can resist Love?
Invincible Love overcomes with power.
You pierce walls and break forts,
Bringing light to the most inaccessible.
You give us strong ardor,
Your wrath subsides and surrenders,
When you dwell in the depths of our heart.
Then Love is the source of our tears.

Powerful Love and sovereign Conqueror,
Whose blows are charming! I love your wounds!
Pull, transform, not sparing my bosom,
Make my blood flow through a thousand openings
Leave nothing behind that is not divine,
Take off impurity, clean the filth,
Banish any broken remnants,
You want your children to have pure souls.

You destroy a heart to make it strong:
Faithfully God moves and animates
Overcoming all without any effort:
This emblem expresses this
As Divine Love guides the bow and arrow for
This fortunate lover;
See how dexterously without perplexity
He shoots the arrow to defeat destiny:
It pierces through this thick and heavy armor:
Nothing can stop love.
Its strength surpasses
The hardest efforts of hell.
Always, Love is stronger than death.

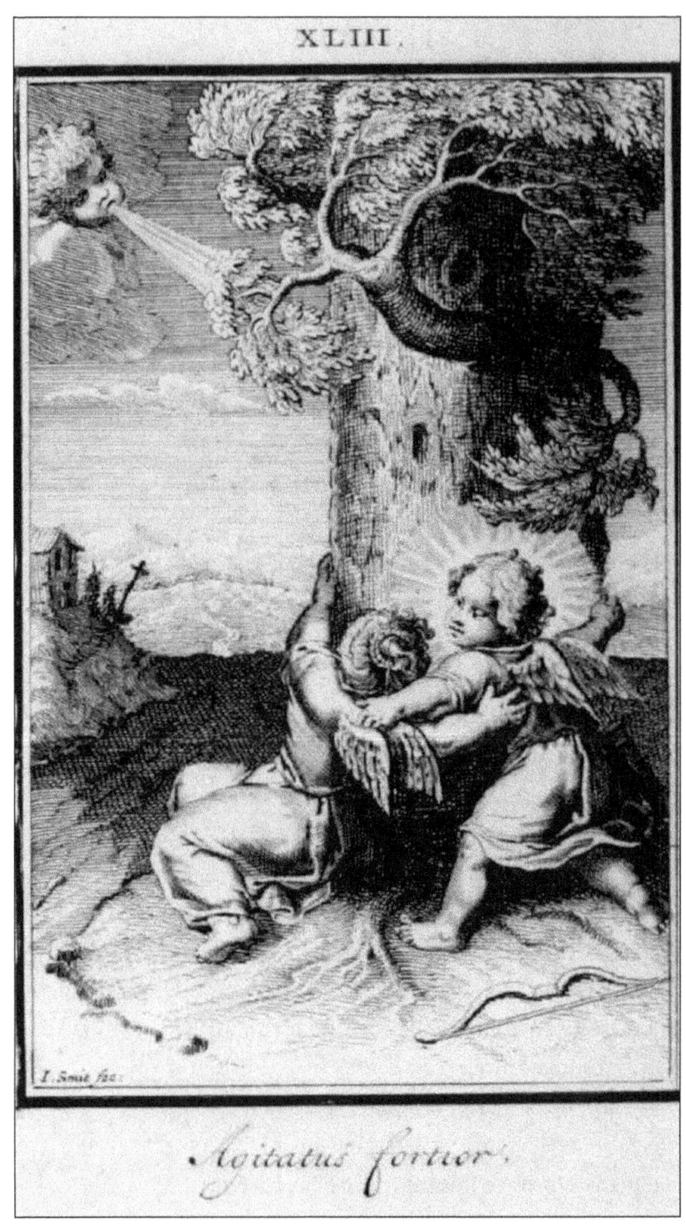

Agitated, she becomes firmer

A face blows a tempest at an oak tree whose branches and leaves twist in the strong gale. Anima sits holding onto the tree, her right arm twined together with the arm of Divine Love. In the background a cross tilts in the storm.

Emblem 43

Agitated, she becomes firmer

The more I am agitated, the more I feel strength;
The tempest only serves to strengthen my interior;
Because my dear Bridegroom condescends to support me,
The evil effects only the outside.

The more I have afflictions, inside I have more
Peace and sweetness: the sovereign Goodness
Appears to bring sorrows
Yet fills me with contentment.

Let envy try to enter me,
I laugh at its futile efforts:
The most painful life and hardest death
Are an infinite good from an infinite source,
By the storm we are led to the port,
Ah, then my soul is ravished!
Then divine strength blesses!

God rewards our struggles.
We know sadness only briefly.
God gives without measure.
Who despises God has only a short and vain happiness.

Holy delights of heaven,
You fill the heart with pleasant ideas;
Your powerful character possesses our souls.
Don't allow us to be moved.
Neither the pleasure of the senses nor frivolous fears,
Can undermine our heart;
We remember that his divine footprints
Make us firm and happy.

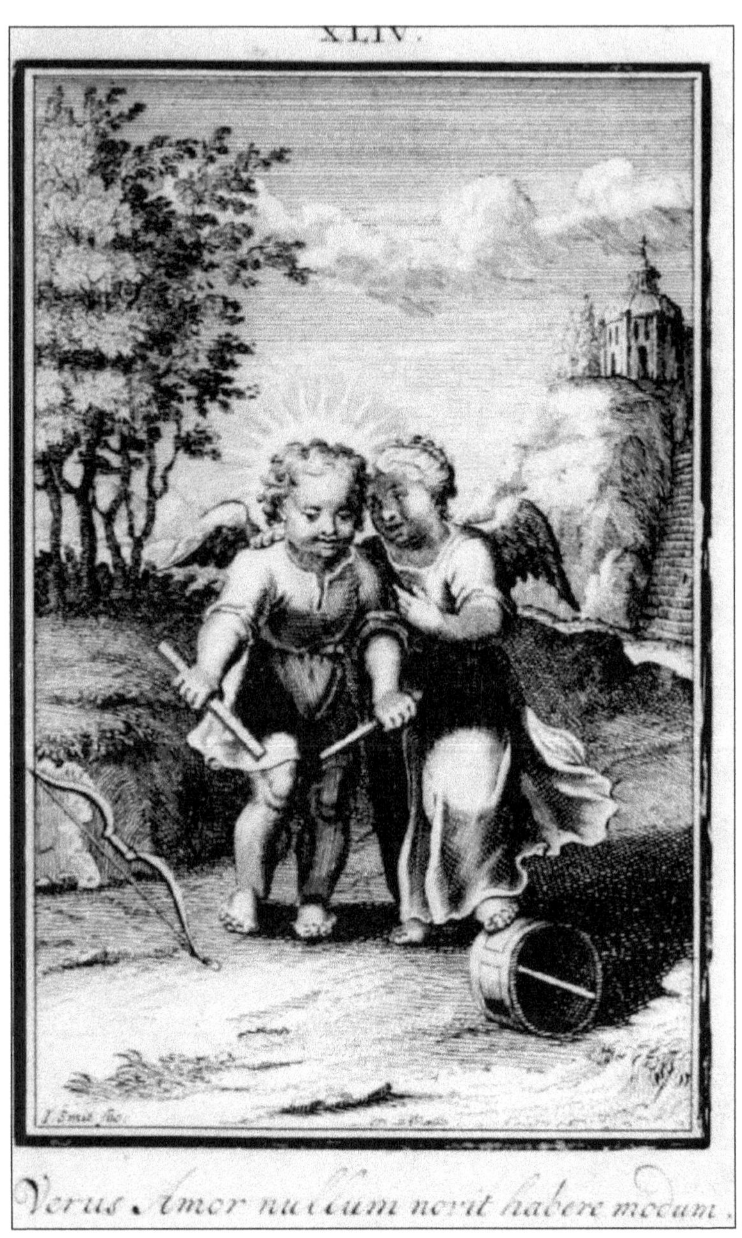

True Love has no measure

With his bow resting on the ground, Divine Love breaks a ruler while Anima, sheltering behind him, whispers in his ear. She rests her left foot on an overturned measuring vessel. In the distance, long stairs lead up to a church with a cross.

Emblem 44

True Love has no measure

Divine Love cannot be measured.
In its divine excess:
Never failing,
It is passionate and powerful!

When we love goodness, we become yielding.
Simple love joined to Truth
Flies effortlessly like an eagle.
Leaving all that is not God,
We want no more of multiplicity.

Oh, when love is intense,
We die to everything, as well as to self,
And there is life in this happy death.
Ah, die always to our own strength!
Then our love becomes sincere and strong,
Inspiring more effort.

Love breaks any spell over my life,
Making me happy and strong.
Love's powerful and strong attractions
Ravish me with mercy.

Love has no limits,
Let us enter the abyss of your love.

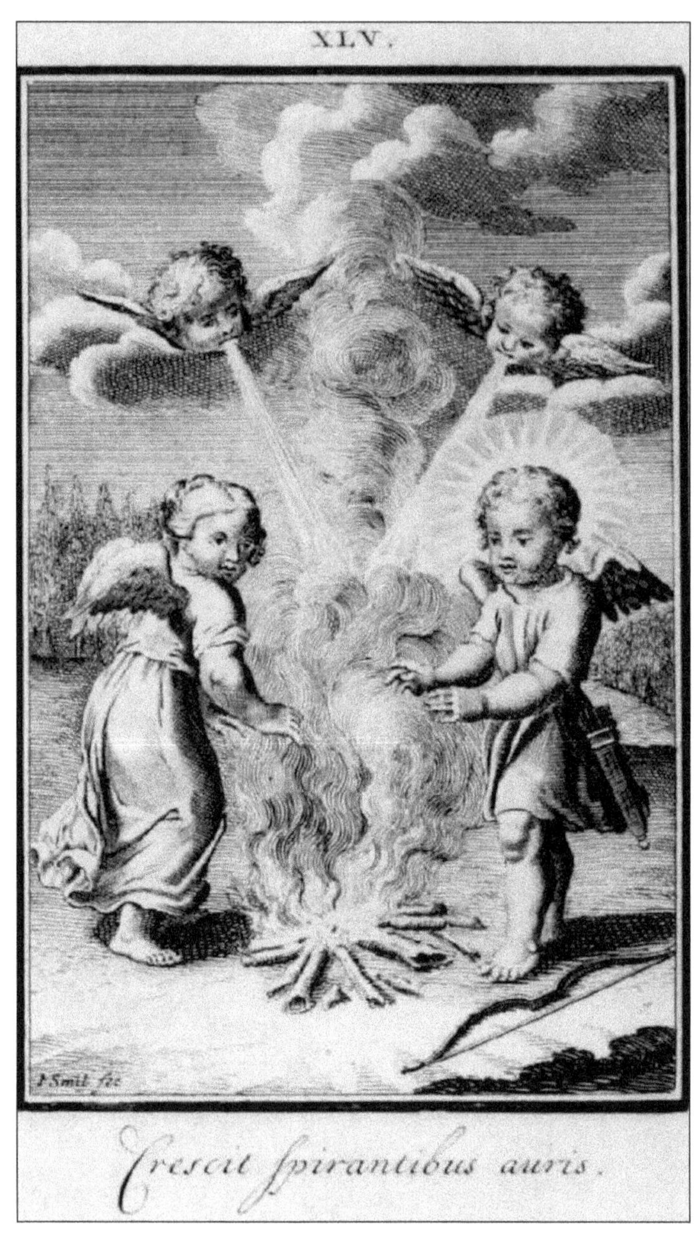

Winds increase

Two faces in the clouds blow winds onto a blazing fire based on crosses of wood. Divine Love and Anima stand across from each by the fire with their hands in the smoke.

Emblem 45

Winds increase

Overwhelmed by ennui and crosses,
I sense in my heart the burning of the sacred fire.
Yet all the horrible torments and many pains,
Far from afflicting me, finally fulfill my desires.

Your divine breath, all adorable Spirit,
That seems to agitate my heart,
Causes inside a delectable calm!
Your Spirit increases my ardor.

Truly your charming love shows me,
Torrents of heavenly pleasures.
Your powerful hand of sovereign Love
With divine generosity fulfills my desires!

Love, Divine Love, who in secret I claim,
Your fires are dear! I adore your rigors.
Ah, if I could one day see your holy flame
Annihilate me and burn more hearts!

Grow, burn without ending, without ever extinguishing
Increasing your torments brings your benefits.
The vehemence of your fire causes no fear.
The more we are consumed, the more we find peace.

O sacred fire, destroy everything and finally destroy my life.
Unite me, I pray you, to my sovereign Good!
I cannot be worthy of envy,
Unless I am reduced to nothing.

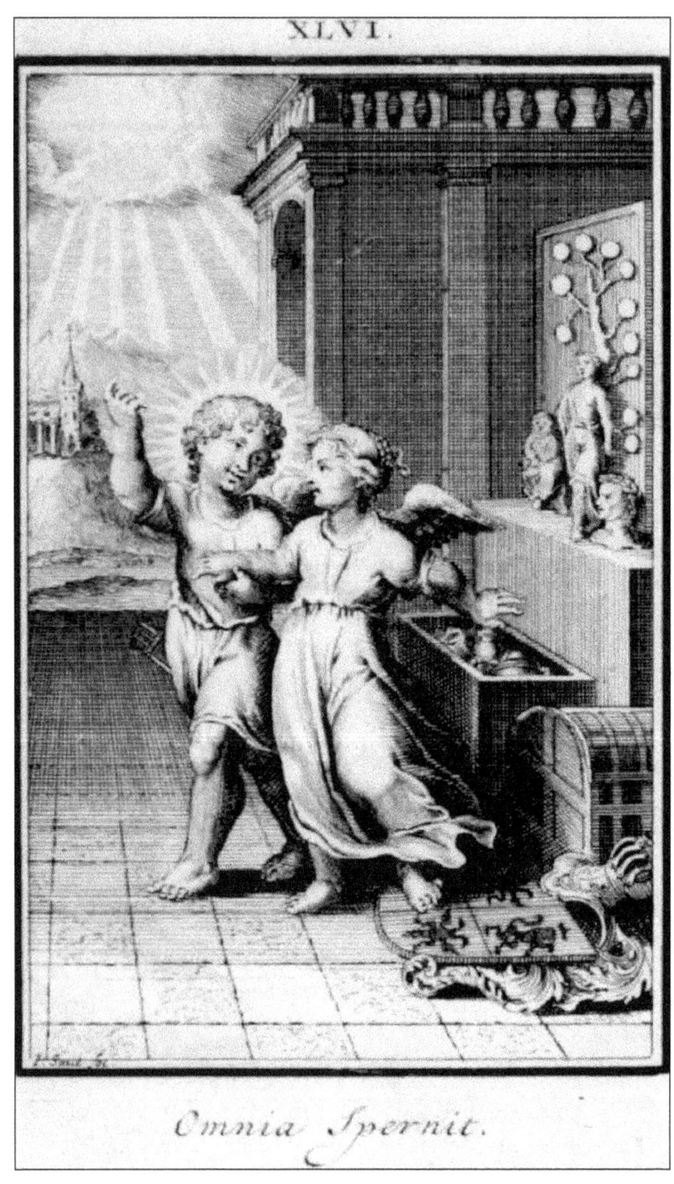

Love disdains all the rest

Holding arms, Divine Love and Anima talk with each other as they leave behind furniture holding many objects: a treasure chest, a chest filled with many things, sculptures of a tall man and a young woman, the bust of a man, a sculpture of a tall tree, among other things.

Emblem 46

Love disdains all the rest

When God is revealed to the heart
Then we have only contempt for
the world's grandeur;
Honors and pleasures only cause
horror;
In leaving everything, we taste
a profound peace,
For we believe that deprivation
Makes true happiness for a soul:
In the midst of contradictions,
We feel the burning of the divine
flame.

Yes, the love of poverty brings
wisdom,
Perfect tranquility, and real wealth.
Happy is the one who possesses
nothing,
Whose clear heart desires nothing
Except our sovereign God!
Because then the heart only aspires
To eternity.
All that we want on earth
Is pure vanity:
Greed only causes trouble.
The poor in spirit cannot fear
The loss of anything.
For what harm can reach us and
what can be taken away?
We have no concern for treasures.
Our only care is to please
Our Lord, whom we love purely:
We think only to satisfy
And make God's pleasure our
contentment.

"Who does not leave everything,"
Jesus said, "to follow me,
Is unworthy of me:
It is far from living
To refuse to die to self.
The world lives and takes pleasure
in everything owned;
Faithful ones live in me only by
deprivation:
I exceed all their desires;
They are fulfilled when I live
in them."

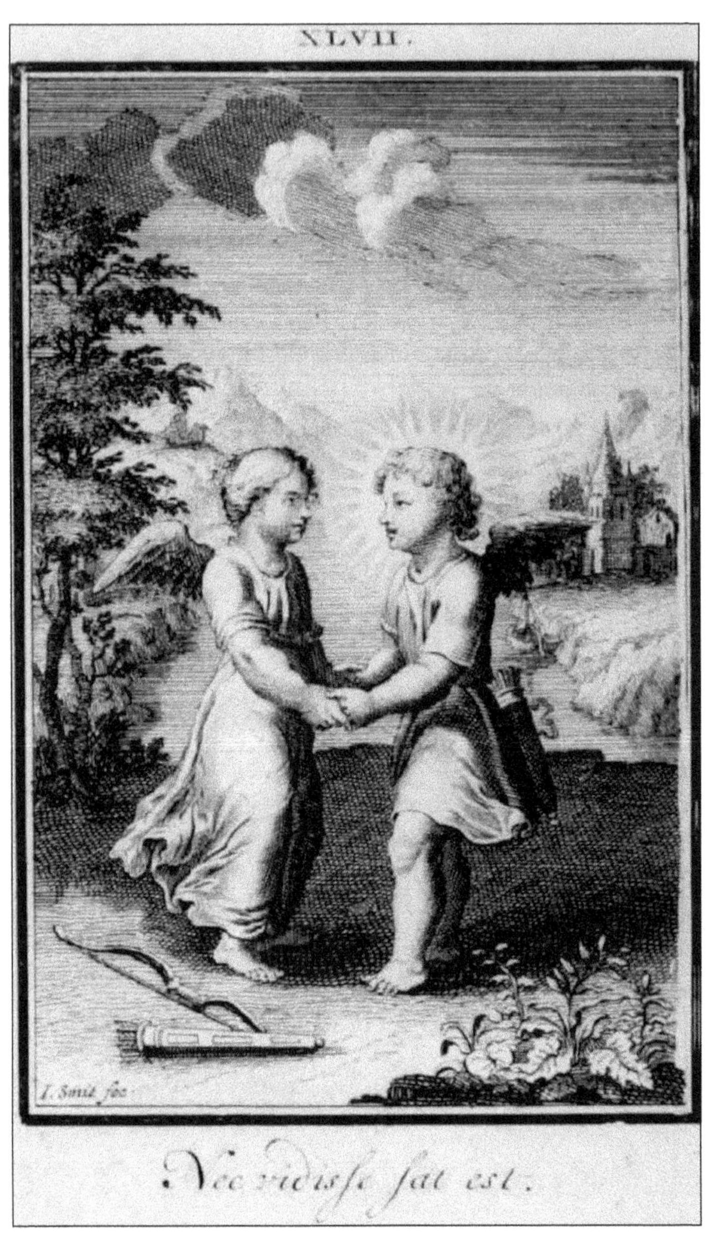

More than seeing

Facing each other directly, Divine Love and Anima hold hands and gaze at the other with satisfaction. In front of them rests the bow and a full quiver of arrows.

Emblem 47

More than seeing

Who can peacefully see you,
Dear Bridegroom of my soul?
In you alone I place my hope,
I burn with pleasure for your holy flame.
What happiness to be entirely filled with you!
I love you, I gaze at you:
My God, these moments are sweet,
And my joy is unparalleled!

The more I see you, the more I am on fire,
Your divine look burns and calms me;
I love you endlessly, I love you eternally,
In my faithfulness I shall find the eternal treasure.

What am I saying? Ah, my transport takes away my judgment,
And I already forget my weakness!
Lord, transform my baseness,
Only you can make me love constantly.

It is also you, dear Bridegroom, who
Shelters my faith through hope;
I know well my misery,
That I have nothing within me.

It is true that Love gives me some daring,
I feel a new courage:
But I depend upon your grace
And your Truth will be my only torch.

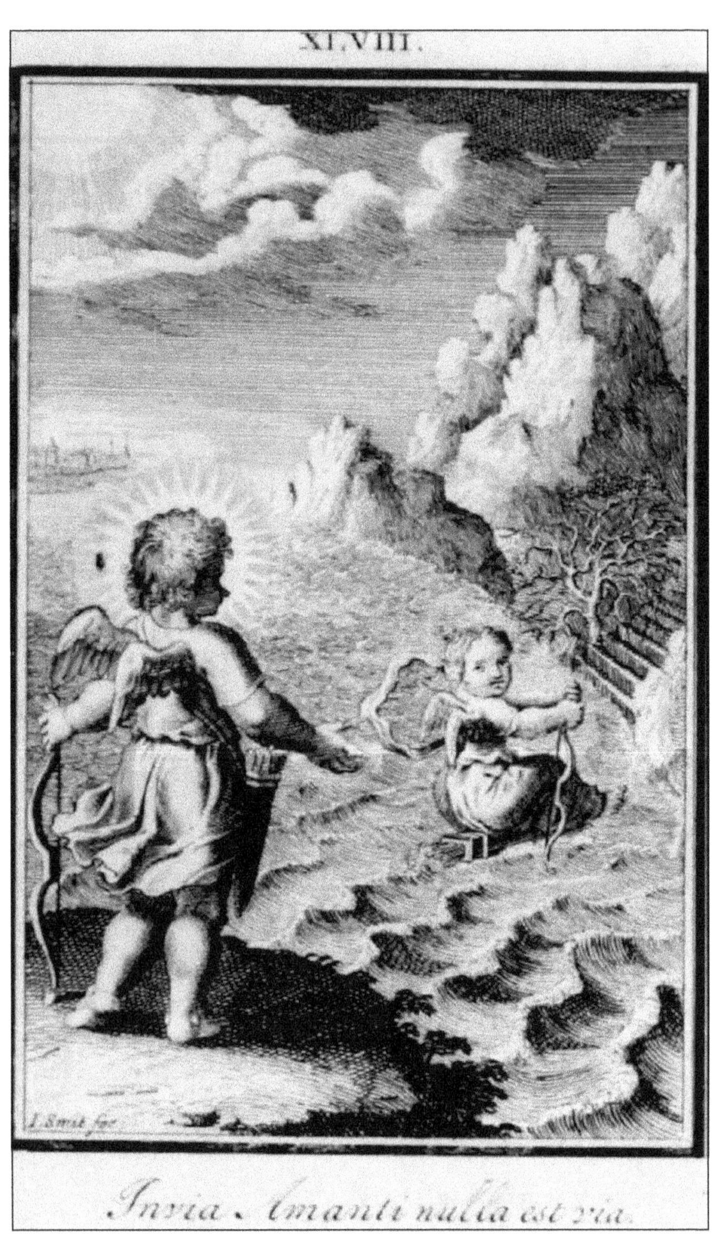

A loving heart can find a way

Lost in a stormy sea, Anima holds onto one single vine. She looks over her shoulder to see Divine Love standing on the beach holding out his hand. Near her an unusual set of stairs climb out of the sea.

Emblem 48

A loving heart can find a way

When we follow Love, we fear no danger.
When we look lost and desolate,
In most dreadful paths, yet the soul finds its way.
We pass through any experience.

This fearless lover traverses through pressures,
The roaring waves of the angry sea,
Without ship or mast: remaining surrendered,
She abandons herself to the care of the Bridegroom.

These terrible pitfalls cause her no trouble,
She disdains to see them:
She finds her repose in the certainty of
His goodness and power.

The less we think about ourselves and the more about Providence
Accompanying us step by step,
We increase our confidence,
His care will not fail us.

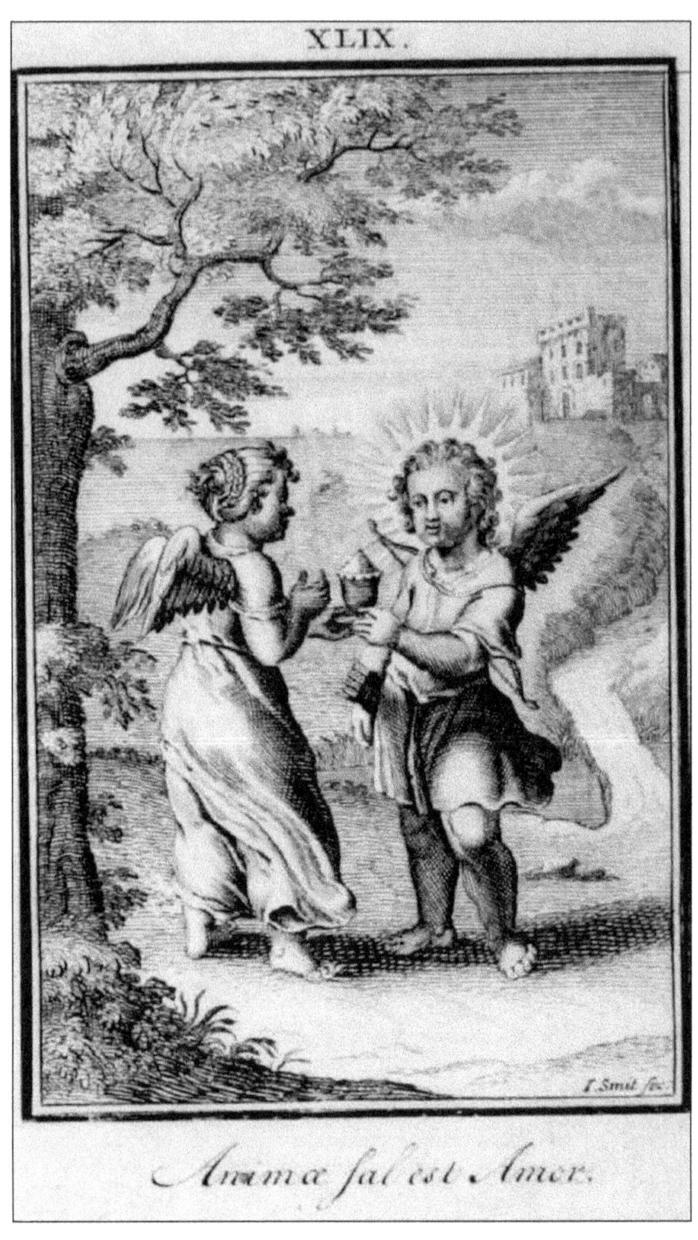

Love is true salt of the soul

Wearing jewels in her hair, Anima and Divine Love jointly hold a small container with a fluted lid. A palace overlooking an ocean rests behind them.

Emblem 49

Love is true salt to the soul

Salt always symbolizes wisdom;
Bringing room for Love's actions,
Making our affections
Both incorruptible and delicate.

Wisdom and Love work well together,
Leading directly to sovereign Good,
And turning the human heart
Away from deceptive charms.

Love, like pure fire, rises to its sphere,
It finds nothing here below
To turn its steps away.
Everything here is poisoned and frustrated.
Love meets death and
With power surpasses death.
Stopping at nothing, Love returns to God;
This admirable fire goes
Back to its source,
Without fault and with purity,
Strength, and repose.

Intense power comes from the salt of wisdom.
Without it, all is insipid and tasteless:
Who does not have this charitable salt, speaks
Without meaning and whose words, like the wind, fade away.
Deceived by false reasoning, without wisdom
The bitter seems sweet and the sweet poison.

Wisdom and Love are the salt of our soul,
They make an exquisite taste.
All good is found here
If we live in the divine flame.

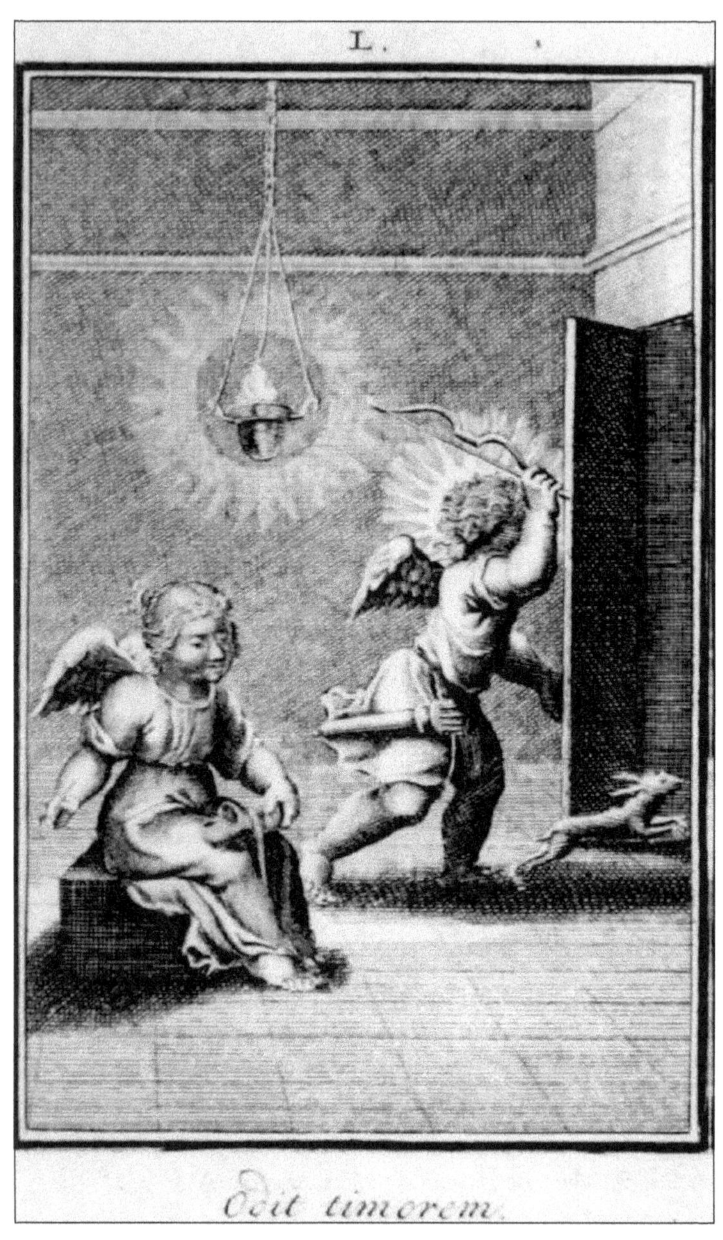

Love chases away all fear

Anima sits while the running Divine Love with a raised bow chases a rabbit out an open door. Overhead a fire burns in a lantern hanging from the ceiling.

Emblem 50

Love chases away all fear

Perfect Love inspires fervor
In its true lovers.
With fear finding no interior place,
Fear itself is banished.

Fear is born of distrust:
When we are filled with faith
We fear nothing;
Pure Love brings faith and trust.

Love elevates and gives us true courage,
Spreading favors
Richly into our enlarged hearts,
Strength is our share.

Our hearts become generous
Our souls become great souls,
We live as places of prudence,
Magnanimous
In all times and places.

Love, Divine Love, gives us largesse;
When our hearts enlarge,
They change into powerful
Enemies of all corruption.

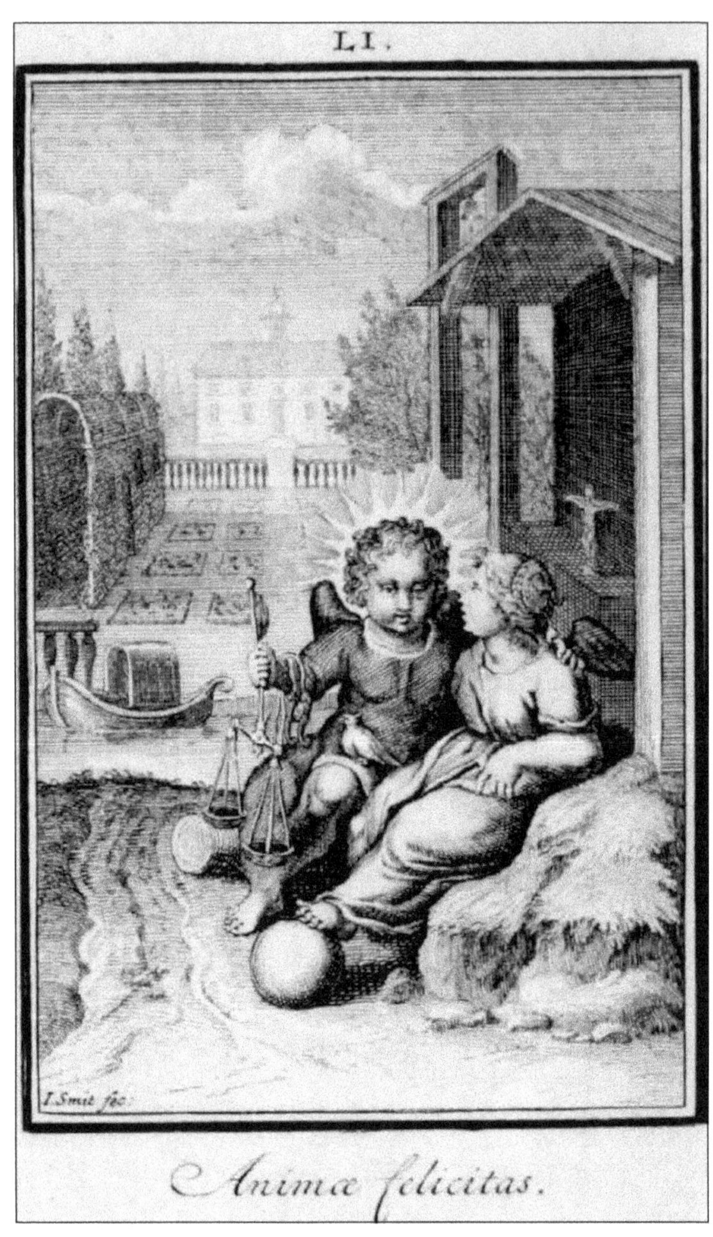

In Love all happiness

Resting in each other's presence, Anima and Divine Love sit and talk while Divine Love holds scales of judgment and Anima rests her foot on a globe. Under a shelter a crucifix appears behind them.

Emblem 51

In Love all happiness

What contentment! The soul
is happy;
How welcome as she tastes
happiness in this place!
Her life is delicious!
And leaving all, unites directly
To this dear Bridegroom whom
her soul desires.
She despises everything that is
not God.

She cares much about how to
please him,
And to satisfy the Bridegroom.
Scorning the world and the flesh,
To make the best approach,
She hides herself
In this solitary place.

There separated from everything
admired,
She shows her fire to her Divine
Lover,
He describes his contentment and
Languor for her sweet martyrdom;
For he is her only love,
For to him her heart lives, moves,
and breathes.

The Bridegroom, charmed by
her wishes, cries
And embraces, rewards well,
By filling her with a thousand
virtues,
He increases her ardor by showing
his charms.
Here all memories are rendered
superfluous,
In this sojourn, happiness banishes
alarms.

Forgetting all about the self,
We abandon ourselves to this
noble ardor:
God possesses the heart.
We taste nothing except this
intense love:
We detest all other honor
Except that of the supreme King;
And our hearts find in him
Strength and support.
Truly he loves.
Love, hope, and faith
Are our only law.

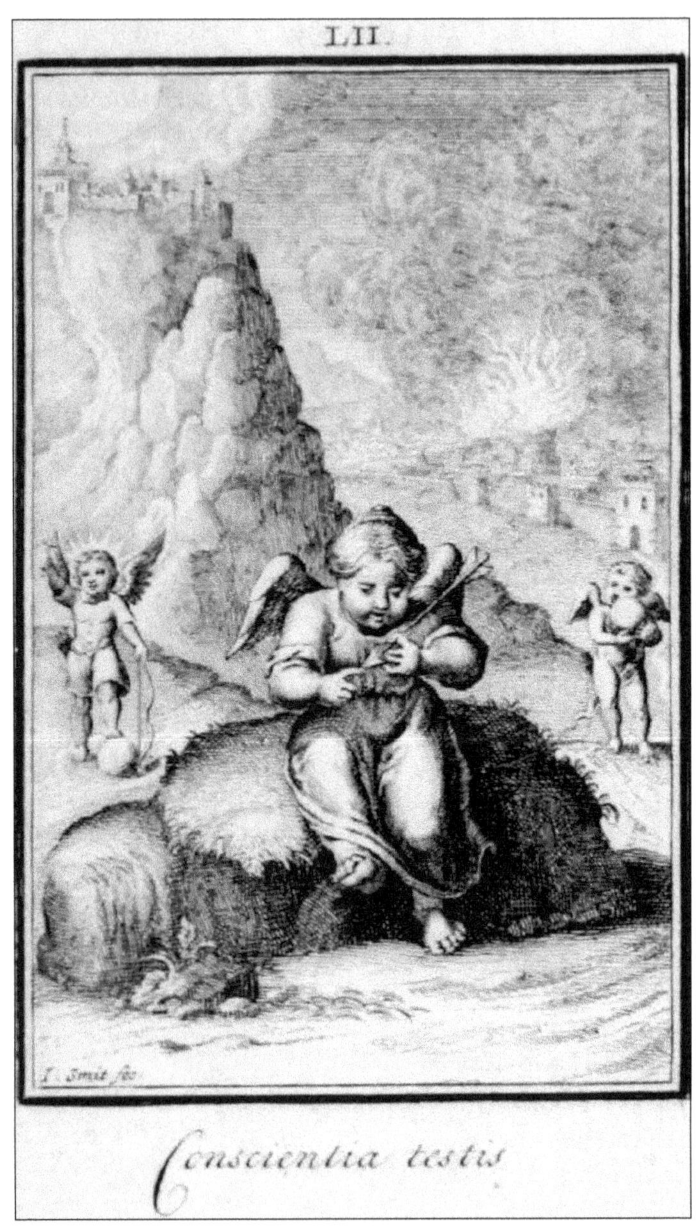

Conscience is witness

Now separated, Divine Love stands in the back with his foot on a globe and a cross in his left hand and his bow in his right. Anima sits in the front and pricks her left hand with an arrow, with the image telling of the prick of conscience.

Emblem 52

Conscience is witness

To listen carefully to what God says to our heart
Is a holy science.
We listen to our conscience with
Its tenderness and pain.

Our conscience is always a faithful counselor,
Certain and never deceptive:
Our self without a conscience becomes cruel
And full of chaotic disorder.

When I follow the voice of conscience, I find tranquility,
My heart is agitated when I do not:
Some profound remorse, a subtle pain,
Makes me feel lost, alas.

All my happiness depends on listening and following;
Woe to those who march over it:
Despite this, the conscience revives
And stifles us with concern.

When following, we no longer feel the burden,
We live content in the sincerity;
And our soul finds largesse,
Living openly in serenity.

God, who has placed this conscience in us, desires that we listen;
It always tells the truth:
And does not leave us in doubt
If we are faithful.

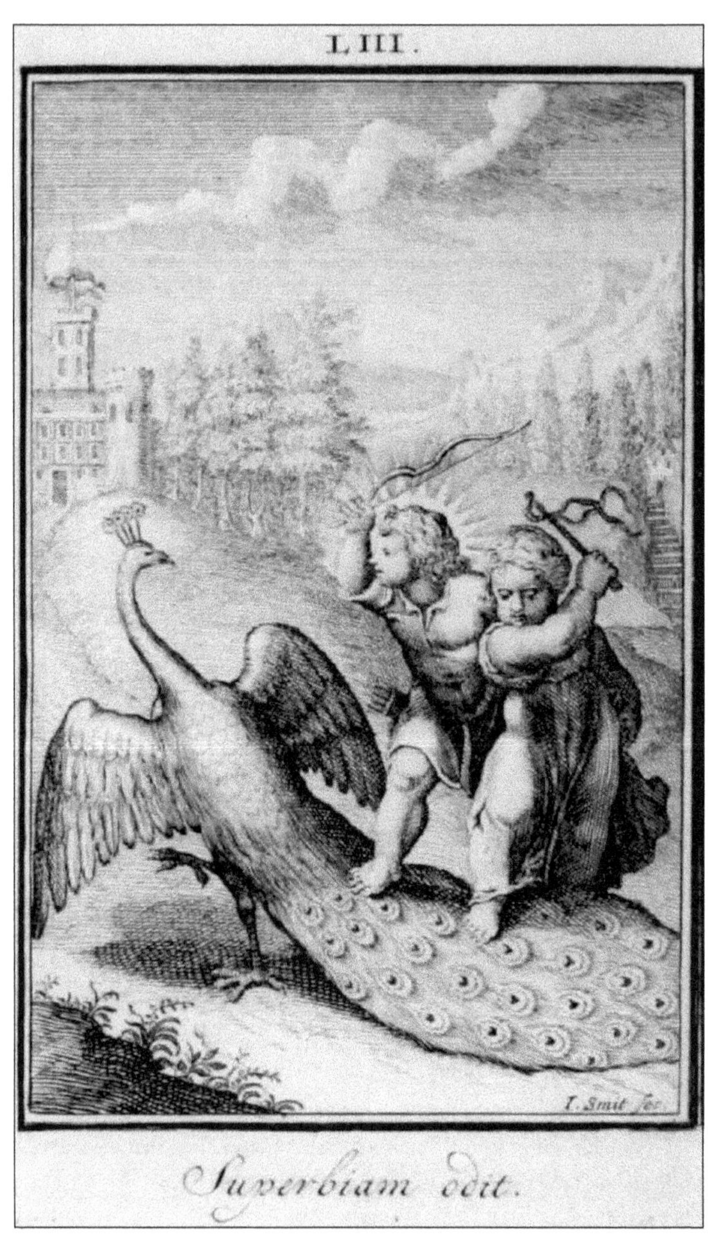

Love abhors pride

A royal peacock processes and both Anima and Divine Love step on its tail. As the peacock turns its head to look at them, Divine Love raises his bow and Anima a stick.

Emblem 53

Love abhors pride

Profound humility
Is the way to God:
God wants us to be nothing,
And not grandly ruling the world.

Jesus Christ first chose humbleness,
His passion chose lowliness,
Poverty, the object of his affection,
Was his doctrine and high wisdom.

Pride only displeases him and banishes our soul,
Haughty ones fill him with horror.
He likes a heart
Humble and pure, enflamed by charity.

Jesus Christ leads and teaches, warms and enlightens,
He never abandons us and gives us
The height of a thousand blessings.
Truly, he loves the humble and small who please him.

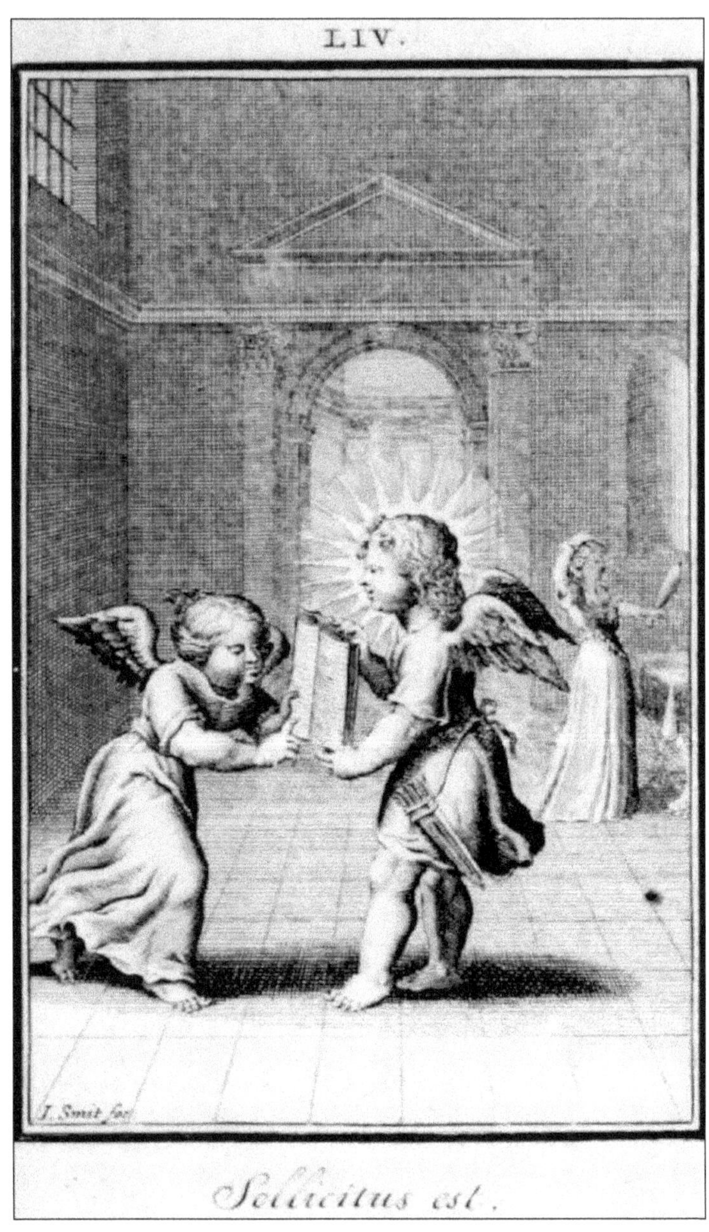

Love carefully teaches the laws

In a tall room where ceilings cannot be seen, Divine Love holds a book that Anima reads. Her finger follows the words, and, listening, she leans into the instruction. In the background a woman stands.

Emblem 54

Love carefully teaches the laws

God's goodness in example
Searches out my error and instructs me,
Opens my eyes and teaches me gently,
And secretly forms God within me.

His divine laws are written in the book.
"This is the purpose," he says, "of your faith:
Listen, leave everything, and follow me;
Practice the counsels and come with me.
Renounce pleasures, embrace virtue
That your heart will not be destroyed by evil,
Die to yourself in order to come alive again.

"Do not tire of admiring and seeing
The excess of my love, and what is my power.
Look at my benefits, listen to my words,
Banish frivolities from your heart,
Think only of pleasing me, and your generous heart
Finds that I only can make you happy.

"Deprived of all goods, you will have abundance:
When misery overwhelms your senses and
Hard labor has filled years,
You taste again my mercy.

"I calm your spirit and relieve your pain,
I soften your troubles and charm your heart.
Against your enemies, I am your only defense.
Nothing can escape my powerful love,
Love me, and let me enter your heart;
Then remain in peace, and in my sure providence."

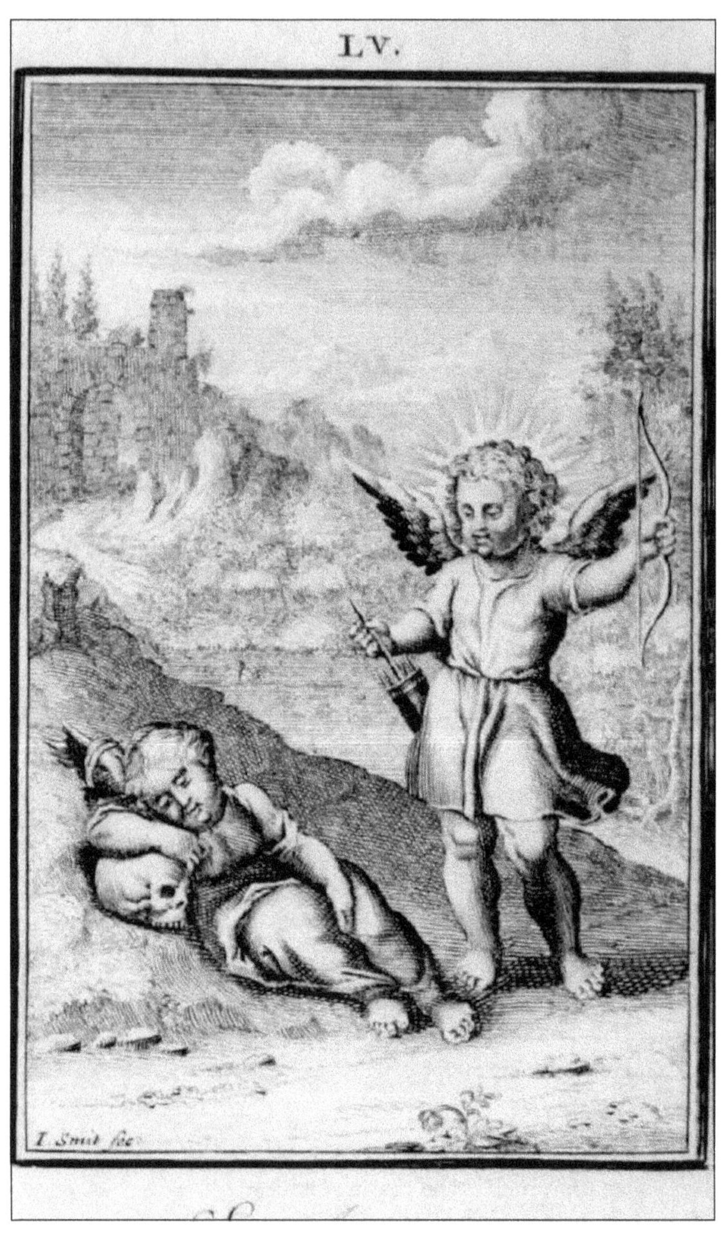

Who does not love remains in death

Anima sleeps while nestling close to a human skull. Divine Love watches over her, holding his bow in one hand and an arrow in the other. The faint scene of a castle rests in the background.

Emblem 55

Who does not love remains in death

Without Divine Love our heart cannot live:
Languishing with cold death,
It cannot by any effort
Rise, hear, and follow.
If the Divine Love touches our miseries
His all-powerful arm takes us
From our weak and languishing state
Where we are first reduced by our sins.

With his unparalleled charity
We seek his solicitude,
With his arrow he touches us.
Injuring our hearts, he opens our ear.

Come, O fire divine, that nothing can douse,
Inflame, inflame my heart;
You alone are the conqueror,
And you only can hit the target.

Only you can wound by your arrows;
It is you, Love, divine Bridegroom!
Do not withdraw;
fill the gap between us.

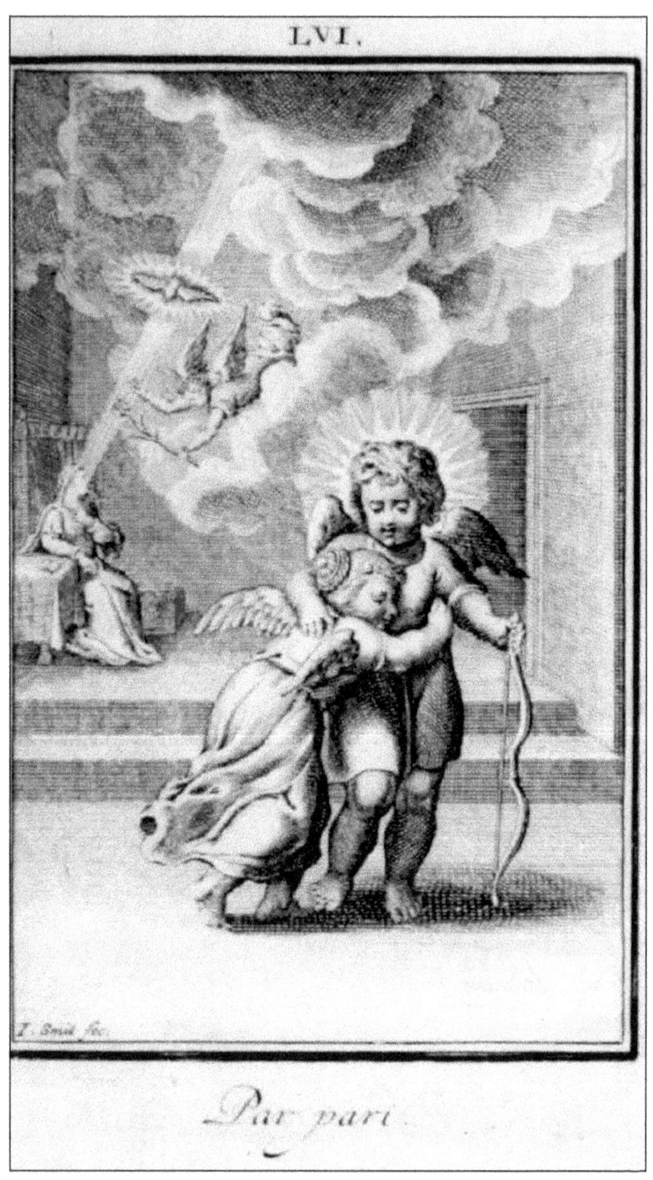

Love reunites the similar

Divine Love and Anima embrace each other. A queen sits on a throne in the background. A bright light shines on her from heaven while the Holy Spirit in the shape of a dove descends in the light, its wings fully extended. An angel offers a branch to her and next to where she sits is a table with a book on it.

Emblem 56

Love reunites the similar

Divine Love fills us with favors:
His caresses are kind!
But to enjoy these delectable goods,
We must give our hearts.

He gives us such strength
Let there be nothing kept in reserve:
When his Love carries us
He gives us his heart and makes our heart his.

He rewards in a moment our troubles and crosses,
He opens his being up to us and dries our tears;
We forget our various pains,
By the effusions of his holy sweetness.

O my Bridegroom, whom I love and I adore,
Be my only support:
I love nothing but you and I desire to
Love you more, O my sovereign Good.

I am all yours, and not for myself,
I never leave you:
The purpose behind my sighs
Is to unite to you by a great love.

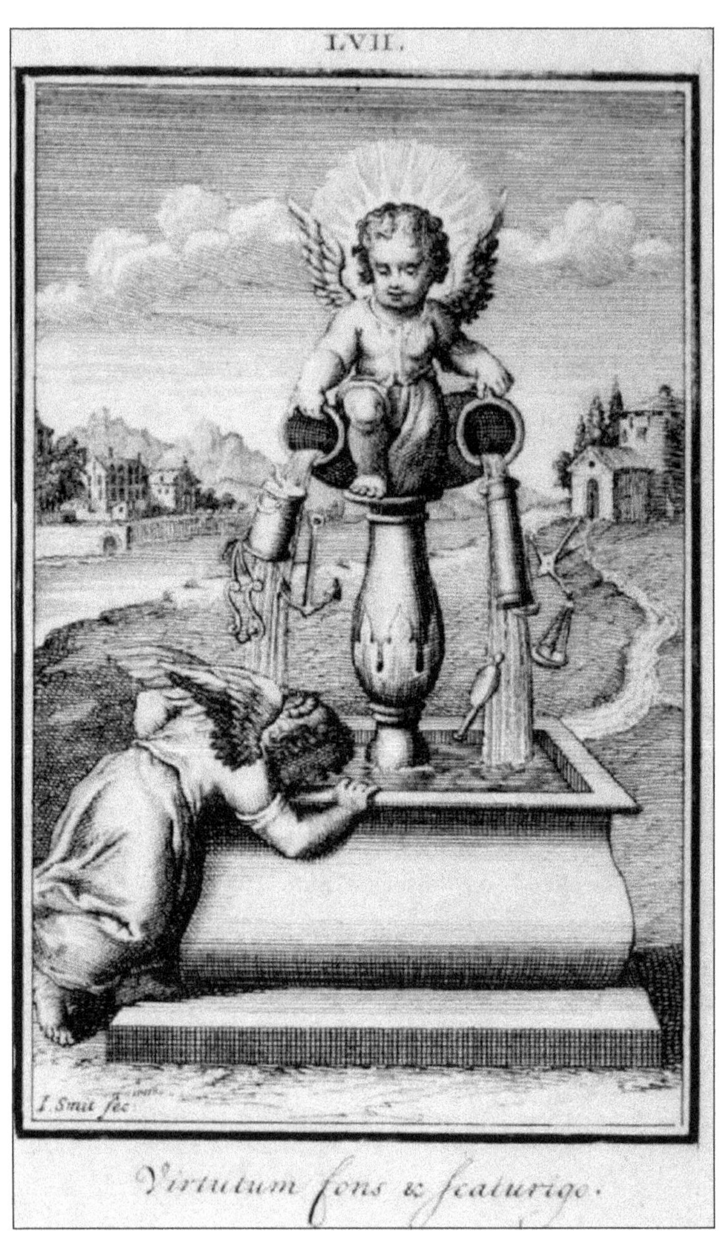

Love is the foundation and support of all virtues

Anima drinks from a fountain, her face almost fully submerged. Divine Love sits on top pouring water into the fountain from two pitchers. Coming out of the pitchers, are also objects: a telescope, scales of judgment, an anchor, and others.

Emblem 57

Love is the foundation and support of all virtues

Flow, divine water, through the mouth of my heart;
I find in you all that I desire,
My heart sighs for the virtues
Given in this sweet liquor.
Faith, charity, all are fruitful,
Hope, humility, strength, and sweetness,
Are found in your waves.

You quench my thirst, I love nothing in the world;
The more I drink you, the more I burn for you:
Fire all divine, source of all fruitfulness,
I taste in you unspeakable goodness.
This excellent beverage
Teaches me a language,
That is little known:
I feel my fire grow,
I am refreshed:
These are admirable mysteries,
This fire is not painful
For my heart in love.

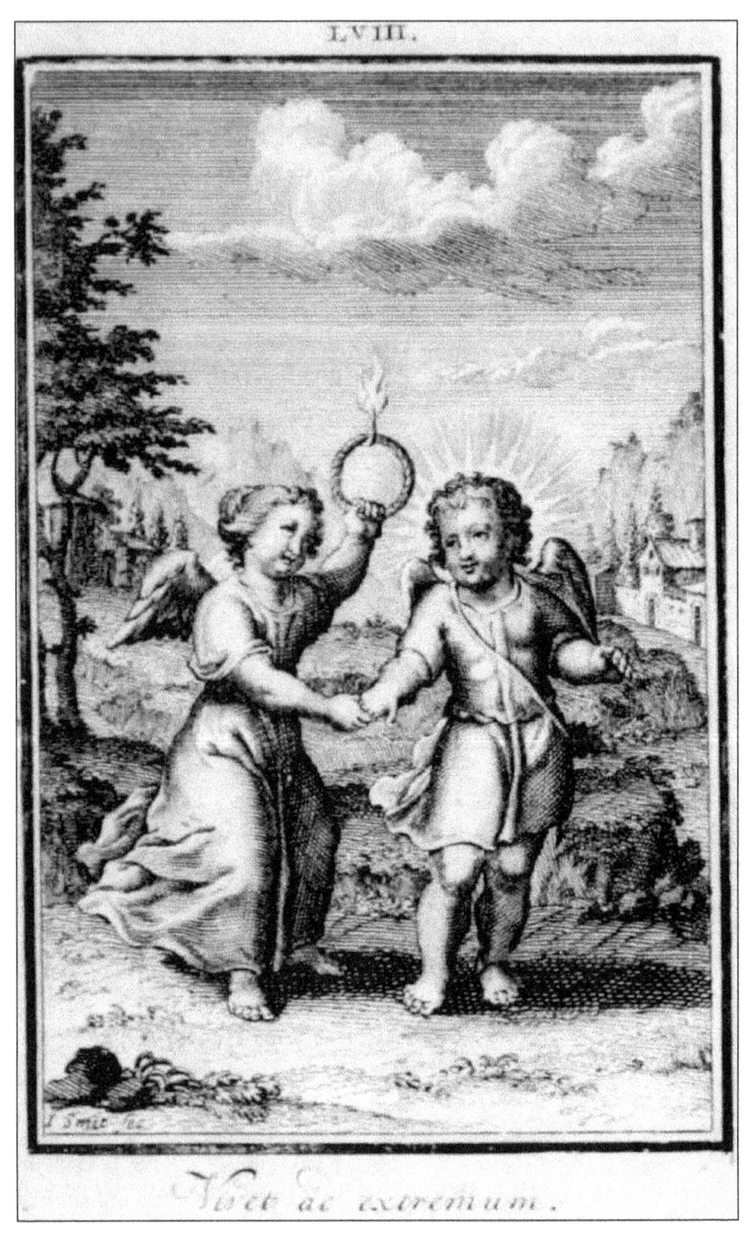

Love lives without ceasing

Anima holds high a ring with a flame coming out of the top of it, while Divine Love and Anima join their right hands.

Emblem 58

Love lives without ceasing

Love that is not pure and divine,
Cannot last a long time: if it captivates our soul,
We see it weaken, change, fade, and finally go out.
It is not so with the celestial flame;
Its eminent character lasts and increases:
Immortality, this sacred Fire,
Burns in time and in eternity,
Its soft warmth heats and enlightens.

It never destroys by burning its subject,
It serves food and preserves life;
The celestial fire is our goal and end,
And causes a holy pleasure that ravishes our soul.

This fire always rises to heaven,
Nothing will make us fall to the side of the earth:
Love possesses the heart, O precious treasure!
This sovereign good is our only concern:
We see everything removed: liberty, property, and honor,
Yet this richness makes us happy for
We admire the divine Wisdom.
We lose only flattering and vain pleasures.

Burn me, fire divine, do not spare my heart,
Broken, crushed, or destroyed, you know the best.
I count for nothing the harshest torments; they are my happiness,
Love, I will please your eyes.

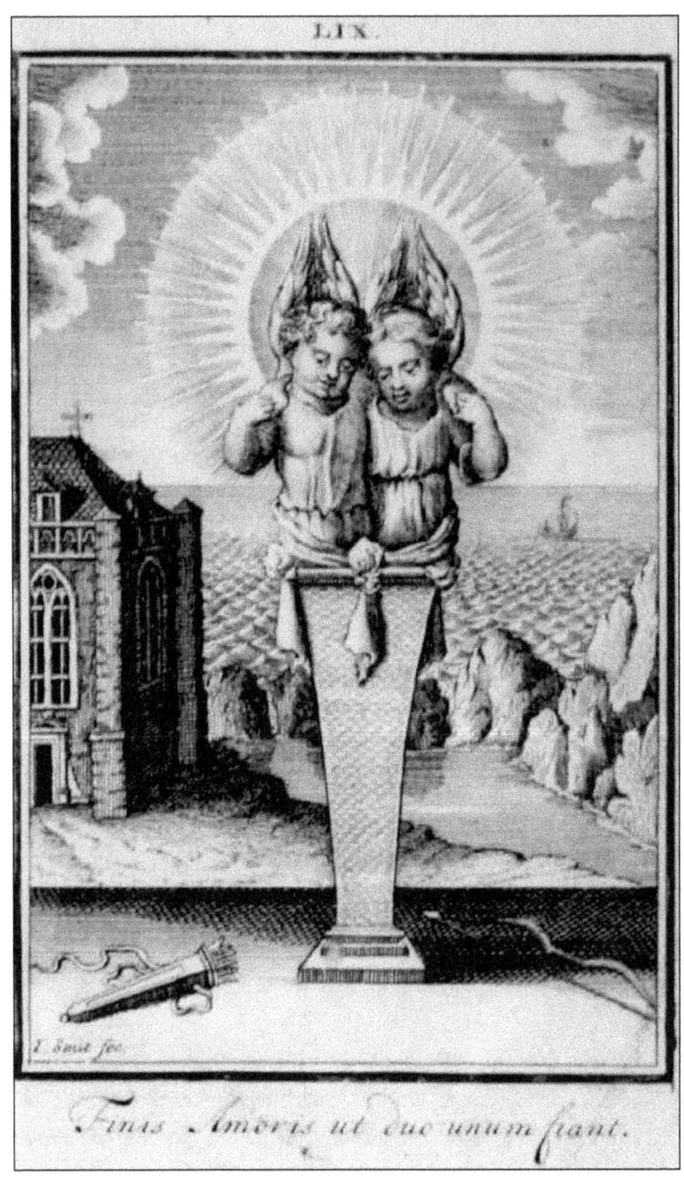

The purpose of Love: the two become one

Kneeling on a tall pedestal, Anima and Divine Love have become united. Their faces with eyes closed appear content and the wings on their backs reach up to heaven. A perfect circle surrounds them. Divine Love's bow and arrows are now cast in front of the pedestal.

Emblem 59

The purpose of Love: the two become one

The end of all things,
The goal of all our desires;
Admirable metamorphosis!
Filling us with innocent pleasures!
The Son asks the Father for union
With his beloved disciples!
Innocent place! Lovely mystery!
Sweet hope of the predestined!

Who could hope for such an advantage,
As you have promised us?
This is the sublime and excellent portion
You give to your friends.

Who could think, or even imagine this?
All the powers of the Spirit blend with nothingness;
The sovereign Lord unites with our little dust,
A drop in the ocean.
He descended to us
To lead us to heaven:
Abandoning his glory, he makes us glorious.
I cannot comprehend
Lord, the greatness of your love.
Permit me to tell you:
I am miserable, unworthy even of the day,
Yet you share with me in your kingdom.

You do still more, you give to me
Your marvelous love.
You transform me into you;
Your kindness astonishes me and fills me with awe.
You offer all who you are,
And I cannot forget this:
I revere what you do.
Happy are those united to you!

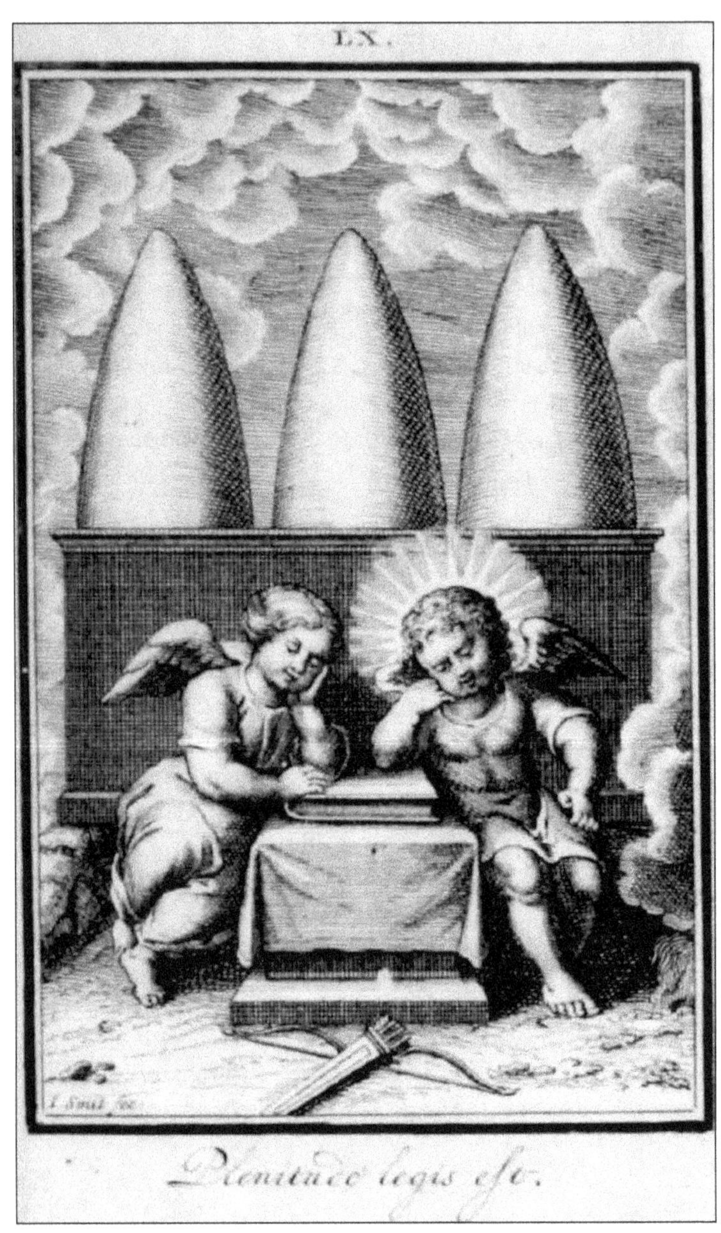

The law of consummation

Sitting at a table, Divine Love and Anima lean on a closed book. In the background three tall prisms, reflecting light, point up to clouds that surround the entire scene. The quiver of arrows has now fallen away.

Emblem 60

The law of consummation

Who can express the extreme happiness
The heart tastes when Love her leads here?
We find a permanent love
Free from ennui, fear, and concern:
All is calm and tranquil,
When we love God only.
We find strong support and a lasting zeal,
We find everything in it: true contentment and
The unchanging peace of which the gospel speaks,
Which passes all understanding,
Making the laws easy,
The united path of right virtues becomes charming.

After the virtues do their work,
We find in Love
This admirable plentitude
Which puts our spirits into truth:
This light easily dispels any cloud
That produces a vain error:
Sacred Love gives the advantage here
To taste celestial sweetness forever.

If you already feel a sweet life,
What should be eternity?
Which exquisite pleasures will fill you?
Unlimited good!
The soul already ravished by God,
Possesses immortality.

Epilogue

You, delight of the pure soul,
Love entering the heart
Has overcome nature
By your pure and chaste ardor;

Light simple, inaccessible,
Sovereign Giver of all good,
You realize the inflexible heart
Destroys itself and becomes nothing inside;

Infant that governs the world,
To whom I dedicate these verses;
For your fruitful grace
Pours into this universe:

Everything comes from knowing you,
From loving you
The only Author of all being
Makes our pure love revered.

Ah, make our love undivided
With a disinterested love;
Make us hear my words,
Love, yes, you have heard me.

I feel stirring hearts,
Receiving from the divine character;
Your pure and naked truth
Touches us and releases our sighs:

I have lived for your glory,
I have desired nothing but you:
Deign to fulfill your victory.
Divine Infant, become our King.

Take away the amusements
And the entertainments,
Deliver us without waiting
Into your all-powerful arms.

To you I implore,
Nothing can hide from you.
O you, whom I love and adore,
We give our hearts.

When we look for you
Without thinking of our own interest;
We live in the supreme will
From which we never depart.

Fix the human inconstancy,
Open to us the secret paths;
Teach us your wisdom,
And deliver us by your holy decrees.

Finally, be the soul of our soul;
Give grace through my song
To produces in us the flame
Which comes from you, divine Infant.

Our Bridegroom is faithful.
If a heart hopes in you.
Your love is eternal,
Favor us with faith.

We sing our adventure
In all songs, in all ways
This love without measure
Surpasses all other gifts.

You caress us
With a thousand chaste pleasures.
All our mutual tenderness
Delight the senses.

Do not believe, faithful people,
That these are only songs:
Under these new figures
Are excellent lessons.

Receive for the divine Master
From my hand these small presents:
For reward, please let us be,
Simple and little children.

END

Selected Bibliography

Daly, Peter M. *Companion to Emblem Studies*. New York: AM, 2008.

Dimler, G. Richard, SJ. "The Jesuit Emblem." In *Companion to Emblem Studies*, edited by Peter M. Daly, 99–128. New York: AMS, 2008.

———. *Studies in the Jesuit Emblem*. New York: AMS, 2007.

Gelderblom, Arie-Jan, Jan L. Dejong, Marc Van Vaeck, eds. *The Low Countries as a Crossroads of Religious Beliefs*. Intersections. Leiden: Brill, 2004.

Gondal, Marie-Louise. *Madame Guyon: un noveau visage*. Paris: Beauchesne, 1989.

Guiderdoni-Duslé, Agnès. "L'ame amante de son Dieu by Madame Guyon (1717): Pure Love between Antwerp, Paris and Amsterdam, at the Crossroads of Orthodoxy and Heterodoxy." In *Intersections*, vol. 3, edited by Arie-Jan Gelderblom, Jan L. de Jong, and Marc van Vaeck, 297–318. Leiden: Brill, 2004.

Guyon, Jeanne. *Ame Amante de son Dieu, representée dans les emblems de Hermannus Hugo sur ses pieux desirs: & dans ceux d'Othon Vaenius sur l'amour divin. Avec des figures nouvelles acompangées de vers qui en font l'aplication aux dispositions les plus essential*. Cologne: Jean de la Pierre, 1717.

James, Nancy Carol. *The Apophatic Mysticism of Madame Guyon*. Ann Arbor, MI: UMI Dissertation Services, 1998.

———. *The Complete Madame Guyon*. Brewster, MA: Paraclete, 2011.

———. *I, Jeanne Guyon*. Jacksonville, FL: Christian Books, 2014.

———. *Jeanne Guyon's Apocalyptic Universe*. Eugene, OR: Pickwick, 2019.

———. *Jeanne Guyon's Christian Worldview*. Eugene, OR: Pickwick, 2017.

———. *Jeanne Guyon's Interior Faith*. Eugene, OR: Pickwick, 2019.

———. *The Pure Love of Madame Guyon*. Lanham, MD: University Press of America, 2007.

———. *The Soul, Lover of God: Emblems by Madame Guyon and Herman Hugo*. Lanham, MD: University Press of America, 2014.

James, Nancy Carol, and Sharon D. Voros. *Bastille Witness: The Prison Autobiography of Madame Guyon (1648–1717)*. Lanham, MD: University Press of America, 2012.

James, William. *The Varieties of Religious Experience*. Reprint, New York: Barnes & Noble Classics, 2004.

Quarles, Francis. *Emblems*. 1635. Delmar, NY: Scholars Facsimiles & Reprints, 1991.

Russell, Daniel. *Emblematic Structures in Renaissance French Culture*. Toronto: University of Toronto Press, 1995.

Veen, Otto van. *Amoris Divini Emblemata*. Antwerp: Balthasaris Moreti, 1615.

www.ingramcontent.com/pod-product-compliance
Lightning Source LLC
LaVergne TN
LVHW020632100826
845148LV00012B/2150

9781532662799